A Passion for

CHOCOLATE

A Passion for

CHOCOLATE

75 Easy Recipes for Chocoholics

JANICE MURFITT

ANAYA PUBLISHERS LTD
LONDON

First published in Great Britain in 1994 by
Anaya Publishers Ltd
Strode House
44–50 Osnaburgh Street
London NW1 3ND

Copyright © Anaya Publishers Ltd 1994

Recipe photography: Alan Newnham
Food stylist: Janice Murfitt
Background artist: Annabel Playfair
Ingredients Photography: Patrick McLeavey
Designer: Patrick McLeavey
Editor: Emma Callery

British Library Cataloguing in Publication Data
Murfitt, Janice
    Passion for Chocolate: 75 Easy Recipes
    for Chocoholics
    I. Title
    641.6

    ISBN 1–85470–112–6

Typeset in Great Britain by Bookworm
Typesetting, Manchester
Colour reproduction by Scantrans Pte Ltd,
Singapore
Printed and bound in Portugal by
Printer Portuguesa Lda

NOTES

Ingredients are listed in metric, imperial
and cup measurements.
Use one set of quantities as they are not
interchangeable.

All spoon measures are level:
1 tablespoon = one 15 ml spoon
1 teaspoon = one 5 ml spoon.

Use standard size 3 eggs unless otherwise
suggested.

CONTENTS

INTRODUCTION

Chocolate is almost irresistible. Dark, rich, smooth and intensely flavoured, it is the perfect accompaniment to any meal. It has an almost addictive quality, making this indulgent ingredient an absolute passion for many people. It also transforms the simplest ingredients into an amalgamation of luxury treats, ranging from simple biscuits (cookies) and cakes to exotic desserts and gâteaux.

Chocolate was first introduced to Europe from the New World by the Spanish in the sixteenth century. At that time it was only used as a drink; eating chocolate wasn't produced until late in the eighteenth century. Today, of course, it is widely used in both confectionary and drinks – and is the perfect ingredient for creating deliciously sweet dishes.

Being a highly processed ingredient, chocolate is an expensive commodity to use. So, to produce the very best results, it is important to understand the different qualities and types of chocolate available. The better the chocolate, the greater the percentage of cocoa butter in the chocolate. If there is less cocoa butter and more added fat, the result can no longer truly be called chocolate. But it is a less expensive alternative for use in cooking.

All chocolate is available as plain (dark), milk (semi-sweet) or white chocolate. Plain (dark) chocolate gives the best flavour as milk (semi-sweet) chocolate is sweeter and softer in texture. White chocolate, being all cocoa butter, has no particular flavour so it is a good base for the addition of flavourings such as fruit zests or juices, coffee or nuts.

The recipes in this book include the use of all types of chocolate as well as cocoa powder, drinking chocolate and chocolate spread. Each chapter is made up of a selection of easy and appealing recipes. These range from cookies and biscuits (how about making *Florentines, Chocolate Shortbread* or *Caramel Bars?*), desserts (*Chocolate and Hazelnut Cloud* or *Chocolate Lime Mousse?*), cakes, pastries and gâteaux (*Chocolate Roulade, Fruit Tartlets* or *Meringue Gâteau?*) to ice creams (*Layered Chocolate Ice Cream* or a *Chocolate Bombe?*), drinks (*Iced Chocolate* or *Chocolate Fruit Frappé?*), sweets (*Rum Truffles* or *Marzipan Cherry Chocolates?*) and finishing touches such as chocolate boxes and baskets.

When making these recipes always ensure the chocolate is fresh for the very best flavour and results. Take care never to let any water, steam or condensation come into contact with melted chocolate and never let the chocolate overheat as it will become granular in texture. Chocolate need not be wasted as leftover melted chocolate may be set and used again at another time.

TOP: Rich chocolate ice cream in a chocolate basket (see pages 29 & 91);
BOTTOM: Dipped chocolates (see page 88).

Chapter 1

PUDDINGS

— *and* —

DESSERTS

Whatever the season, in this chapter there's a tempting chocolate dessert that's just right. You might choose a warming chocolate sponge pudding floating in a rich sauce, or a light-textured fruit omelette in the winter. Lightly whipped chocolate mousses and smooth, refreshing creams are perfect for warmer days.

For those special occasions, delight your guests with the impressive *Charlotte Russe* or *Clementines in Chocolate Sauce*. If you are really short of time, choose one of the ultra-quick whips – such as *Chocolate Zabaione* or *Hazelnut Cloud*. This has a speedy topping which is equally suitable for filling cakes, gâteaux and pastries.

CHOCOLATE & HAZELNUT CLOUD

SERVES 4–6

Fresh fruits with a simple, quick chocolate topping – made in minutes. Use any fruits, and add Madeira or brandy for extra zing.

125 g (4 oz) fresh pineapple, peeled and cored
125 g (4 oz) strawberries, hulled
125 g (4 oz) seedless grapes
2 tablespoons orange juice
TOPPING
150 ml (5 fl oz/²⁄₃ cup) whipping cream
4 tablespoons chocolate hazelnut spread
4 tablespoons thick Greek yogurt
TO DECORATE
strawberry leaves

1 Cut the fruit into small pieces and place in a bowl with the orange juice; mix gently.

2 Divide the fruit equally between 4 or 6 glasses, reserving a few pieces for decoration.

3 For the topping, whisk the cream and chocolate hazelnut spread together until thick enough to hold its shape. Fold in 2 tablespoons of the yogurt until evenly blended.

4 Spoon the topping over the fruit.

5 Spoon the remaining yogurt on top and decorate with the reserved fruit and strawberry leaves.

CHOCOLATE LIME MOUSSE

MAKES 8

The tang of lime lightens the richness of chocolate to delicious effect. Try orange or lemon if you prefer.

4 eggs, separated
90 g (3 oz) caster (superfine) sugar
185 g (6 oz/¹⁄₃ cup) white chocolate, melted
finely grated rind and juice of 2 limes
2 teaspoons powdered gelatine
TO DECORATE
lime rind shreds
chocolate curls

1 Place the egg yolks and sugar in a heatproof bowl over a saucepan of simmering water and whisk until thick and pale. Remove the bowl from the heat and stir in the chocolate, lime rind and juice.

2 Soften the gelatine in 2 tablespoons water. Place over the saucepan of hot water until dissolved.

3 Stir the gelatine into the lime mixture and chill for 2-3 minutes until the mixture begins to thicken.

4 Whisk the egg whites in a clean bowl until stiff. Gradually add to the lime mixture, carefully folding in after each addition.

5 Pour the mixture into 6 tall glasses or individual dishes and leave to set.

6 Decorate each mousse with shredded lime rind and chocolate curls.

FRONT: Chocolate & hazelnut cloud; BACK: Chocolate lime mousse.

CHOCOLATE ZABAIONE

SERVES 4–6

3 egg yolks
85 ml (3 fl oz/¹/₃ cup) chocolate cream liqueur
30 g (1 oz/5 teaspoons) caster (superfine)
  sugar
1 tablespoon chocolate spread

1 Place the egg yolks, chocolate liqueur and sugar in a heatproof bowl over a saucepan of simmering water.

2 Whisk continuously with an electric whisk for about 10 minutes until the mixture is thick and pale, and leaves a trail when the whisk is lifted.

3 Remove the bowl from the saucepan and continue whisking for a few minutes.

4 Divide between 4 or 6 tall glasses. Drizzle a little chocolate spread into each glass and swirl with a cocktail stick.

5 Serve warm or cold, with dessert biscuits if desired.

MOCHA VELVET

SERVES 6

125 g (4 oz) white chocolate
125 g (4 oz) milk (semi-sweet) chocolate
3 passion fruit
1 teaspoon coffee granules
250 g (8 oz) fromage frais
TO DECORATE
chocolate curls

1 Melt the white and milk (semi-sweet) chocolate in separate bowls.

2 Halve the passion fruit and scrape the seeds and flesh into a sieve over a bowl. Using a wooden spoon, press all the juice through, discarding the seeds.

3 In a small bowl, dissolve the coffee granules in 1 tablespoon boiling water.

4 Add the passion fruit juice and half of the fromage frais to the white chocolate. Stir until smooth.

5 Add the coffee and the remaining fromage frais to the milk chocolate, stirring until well blended.

6 Fill 6 individual glass dishes with alternate spoonfuls of white chocolate and mocha mixture. Leave in a cool place to set.

7 Decorate with chocolate curls to serve.

FRONT: Mocha velvet; BACK: Chocolate zabaione.

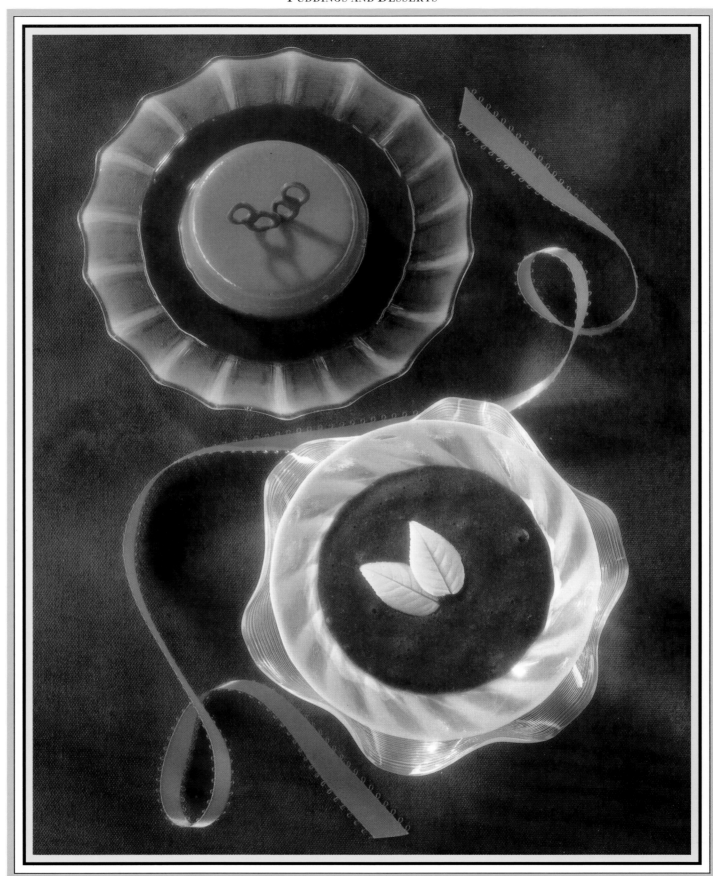

CHOCOLATE CREAMS

MAKES 6

550 ml (20 fl oz/2½ cups) milk
125 g (4 oz) plain (dark) chocolate, in pieces
2 eggs
2 egg yolks
25 g (1 oz/5 teaspoons) caster (superfine)
  sugar
CHOCOLATE SAUCE
150 ml (5 fl oz/⅔ cup) single (light) cream
60 g (2 oz) plain (dark) chocolate, in pieces
TO DECORATE
piped chocolate designs or curls

1 Pre-heat the oven to 170°/325°F/Gas 3.
Place 6 individual soufflé dishes in a roasting
tin (pan). Half fill with hot water.

2 Place the milk and chocolate in a saucepan
and heat gently until melted.

3 Meanwhile, whisk the eggs, egg yolks and
sugar together in a heatproof bowl.

4 Pour the chocolate milk on to the eggs,
whisking constantly. Strain into a jug.

5 Fill each soufflé dish with chocolate custard
and cover the tin (pan) with a piece of foil.
Bake in the oven for 30–35 minutes, or until
set. Leave until cold.

6 Meanwhile, make the chocolate sauce.
Gently heat the cream and chocolate in a small
pan until the chocolate has melted. Bring to
the boil, then pour into a jug.

7 Loosen the edge of each chocolate cream and
invert on to a small serving plate.

8 Pour the sauce around the chocolate
creams. Top with chocolate designs or curls.

CHOCOLATE RUM MOUSSE

MAKES 6

A light-textured mousse with the addition of
yogurt or fromage frais. For children, replace
the rum with fruit juice, and use milk
chocolate.

185 g (6 oz) plain (dark) chocolate
15 g (½ oz) unsalted butter
3 eggs, separated
2 tablespoons dark rum
6 tablespoons thick Greek yogurt
TO DECORATE
white chocolate leaves or cut-outs

1 Break up the chocolate and place in a
heatproof bowl with the butter over a
saucepan of hot water. Stir occasionally, using
a wooden spoon, until melted.

2 Stir in the egg yolks and rum until smooth.
Add the yogurt and stir until evenly blended.

3 Whisk the egg whites in a clean bowl until
stiff. Gradually add to the chocolate mixture,
carefully folding in after each addition, until
the mixture is evenly blended.

4 Divide the mixture between 6 small dishes
and leave to set.

5 Decorate with chocolate leaves or cut-outs
just before serving.

TOP: Chocolate creams; BOTTOM: Chocolate rum mousse.

CHOCOLATE RUSSE

SERVES 6

A rich, tempting dessert for a special occasion. Use cherries, redcurrants, blueberries, raspberries or strawberries.

1 packet (16) sponge fingers
FILLING
250 g (8 oz) milk (semi-sweet) chocolate, melted
3 eggs, separated
2 tablespoons Marsala or orange juice
125 g (4 oz) cream cheese
150 ml (5 fl oz/²⁄₃ cup) single (light) cream
TO DECORATE
150 ml (5 fl oz/²⁄₃ cup) whipping cream, whipped
125 g (4 oz) soft fruit

1 Line the base of a 15 cm (6 in) charlotte mould or soufflé dish with baking parchment. Arrange the sponge fingers around the inside of the dish, trimming them level with the top.

2 Stir the egg yolks and Marsala or orange juice into the chocolate until smooth.

3 In a separate bowl, beat the cream cheese and single (light) cream until smooth. Stir into the chocolate mixture. Leave to thicken.

4 Whisk the egg whites in a clean bowl until stiff. Gradually add to the chocolate mixture, folding in after each addition.

5 Pour the mixture into the mould and leave to set.

6 Just before serving, invert on to a serving plate and remove lining paper. Decorate with piped cream and soft fruit.

CHOCOLATE TRIFLE LAYER

SERVES 6

185 g (6 oz) plain (dark) or milk (semi-sweet) chocolate, melted
90 g (3 oz) plain cake, crumbled
2 tablespoons crème de framboise liqueur or kirsch
150 ml (5 fl oz/²⁄₃ cup) whipping cream
2 tablespoons thick Greek yogurt
185 g (6 oz/1¼ cups) raspberries, hulled
TO DECORATE
chocolate cut-outs

1 Line a baking sheet with baking parchment.

2 Pour the chocolate over the paper-lined baking sheet and spread evenly to cover, using a palette knife. Pick up the top two corners of the paper and drop several times to level the chocolate and smooth the surface. Leave until the chocolate is almost set but still pliable.

3 Lay a clean piece of baking parchment over the surface and invert the chocolate on to it. Peel the paper off the back of the chocolate and turn the chocolate over.

4 Using a ruler and a sharp knife, cut 12 7.5 cm (3 in) squares.

5 Mix the cake crumbs and liqueur together.

6 In a separate bowl whip the cream and yogurt together until thick.

7 Place a chocolate square on each serving plate and pipe on one third of the cream. Cover with the crumb mixture and top with remaining chocolate squares.

8 Pipe another one third of cream, and cover with raspberries. Add a swirl of cream to each and decorate with chocolate cut-outs.

TOP: Chocolate russe; BOTTOM: Chocolate trifle layer.

CHOCOLATE SAUCE PUDDING

SERVES 4

50 g (3 oz/¹⁄₃ cup) soft margarine
90 g (3 oz/¹⁄₃ cup) soft light brown sugar
90 g (3 oz/¹⁄₃ cup) self-raising wholemeal flour
1 tablespoon cocoa powder
2 eggs
30 g (1 oz/¹⁄₄ cup) pecan nuts, chopped
30 g (1 oz/¹⁄₄ cup) raisins
CHOCOLATE SAUCE
1 tablespoon cocoa powder
1 tablespoon cornflour (cornstarch)
1 tablespoon soft light brown sugar
300 ml (10 fl oz/1¹⁄₄ cups) boiling water
TO SERVE
icing (confectioner's) sugar for dusting

1 Preheat oven to 180°C (350°F/Gas 4). Lightly butter a 1.2 litre (2 pint) shallow ovenproof dish.

2 In a mixing bowl, beat the margarine, sugar, flour, cocoa powder and eggs together, using an electric mixer for 1-2 minutes or wooden spoon for 2-3 minutes until smooth and glossy.

3 Stir in the nuts and raisins, then spoon into the prepared dish. Smooth the top.

4 For the sauce, blend the cocoa, cornflour (cornstarch) and sugar together with 2 tablespoons cold water. Add the boiling water, stirring, until smooth.

5 Pour the sauce over the pudding mixture and bake for 40-45 minutes until well risen and springy to the touch.

6 Dust with icing (confectioner's) sugar; serve with cream.

CHOCOLATE SOUFFLE OMELETTE

SERVES 4

Fill the omelette with any seasonal fruit.

4 eggs, separated
1 teaspoon caster (superfine) sugar
2 tablespoons chocolate cream liqueur
15 g (¹⁄₂ oz/3 teaspoons) butter
1 tablespoon chocolate spread
1 orange, segmented
TO DECORATE
icing (confectioner's) sugar for dusting
mint leaves and orange rind shreds

1 Place the egg yolks, sugar and liqueur in a bowl. Whisk until thoroughly blended.

2 Whisk the egg whites with clean beaters until stiff, then gradually add to the egg yolk mixture, carefully folding in after each addition until evenly blended.

3 Preheat the grill to high. Melt the butter in a 20 cm (8 in) omelette pan until hot. Quickly add the omelette mixture and cook for 2-3 minutes or until the underside is golden brown.

4 Place the omelette under the grill for 1-2 minutes until golden brown on top.

5 Slide the omelette on to a warmed plate. Drizzle with chocolate spread and place the orange segments on one half.

6 Fold the omelette over the oranges and dust with icing (confectioner's) sugar. Decorate with mint leaves and orange shreds. Serve immediately.

TOP: Chocolate sauce pudding;
BOTTOM: Chocolate soufflé omelette.

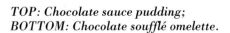

SPICY FRUIT CREPES

SERVES 4-6

500 g (3½ oz) plain (all purpose) flour
15 g (½ oz/2 tablespoons) cocoa powder
1 egg
300 ml (10 fl oz/1¼ cups) milk and water
*   mixed*
oil for frying
FRUIT FILLING
150 ml (5 fl oz/⅔ cup) water
5 cm (2 in) cinnamon stick
125 g (4 oz/½ cup) caster (superfine) sugar
4 plums, stoned and thinly sliced
2 small bananas, thickly sliced
TO DECORATE
icing (confectioner's) sugar for dusting
lemon geranium leaves

1 Sift the flour and cocoa powder into a bowl. Make a well in the centre and add the egg and half of the milk and water mixture. Using a wooden spoon, beat until smooth. Stir in the remaining liquid. Alternatively, place all the ingredients in a food processor and work for 1 minute. Pour into a jug.

2 Heat a little oil in a 15 cm (6 in) frying pan. Pour in a little of the batter and swirl to coat the base evenly.

3 Cook until the edge of the crêpe begins to leave the side of the pan. Turn and cook the underside until crisp. Place on a warmed plate. Repeat to make 12 crêpes stacking them interleaved with greaseproof (waxed) paper as they are cooked; keep warm.

4 To prepare the fruit filling, place the water and cinnamon in a saucepan. Bring to the boil. Stir in the sugar, then add the fruit and bring to the boil. Remove from the heat and let stand for 1 minute.

5 Remove the fruit with a slotted spoon and arrange on one half of each crêpe. Fold crêpes in half, then quarters. Arrange on serving plates.

TOP: Frosted chocolate crêpes;
BOTTOM: Spicy fruit crêpes.

6 Bring the syrup to the boil and boil rapidly for 1 minute. Discard the cinnamon and pour the syrup over the crêpes.

7 Dust with icing sugar and decorate with lemon geranium leaves to serve.

FROSTED CHOCOLATE CREPES

SERVES 4-6

12 chocolate crêpes (see left)
60 g (2 oz) plain (dark) chocolate
150 ml (5 fl oz/⅔ cup) single (light) cream
icing (confectioner's) sugar for dusting
12 scoops of ice cream
TO DECORATE
chocolate curls

1 Gently heat the chocolate and cream in a small pan, stirring occasionally, until melted.

2 Dust the warm crêpes with icing sugar and fold into triangles. Arrange on individual serving plates.

3 Pour a pool of sauce on to each plate and arrange the ice cream scoops and chocolate curls on top just before serving.

CLEMENTINES IN CHOCOLATE SAUCE

SERVES 4

1 tiny clementines
1 large orange
125 g (4 oz/¹/₂ cup) caster (superfine) sugar
60 g (2 oz) plain (dark) chocolate
1 tablespoon orange curaçao or cointreau
3 tablespoons whipping cream
TO DECORATE
clementine leaves

1 Peel the clementines, removing the white pith from the outside and centre, keeping the fruit whole.

2 Using a canelle knife, pare the rind from the orange into thin shreds.

3 Squeeze the juice from the orange and place in a saucepan with the sugar and orange shreds. Heat gently until the sugar has dissolved, then boil for 30 seconds.

4 Remove the orange shreds with a slotted spoon, then place the clementines in the syrup and bring to the boil. Cover and cook gently for 3-4 minutes until clementines look translucent; remove with slotted spoon.

5 Add the chocolate to the syrup; stir until melted. Stir in the liqueur and 2 tablespoons cream.

6 Pour a pool of chocolate sauce on to each serving plate and place 3 clementines in the centre. Decorate with orange shreds and clementine leaves.

7 Just before serving, drop dots of cream on to the chocolate sauce and draw a cocktail stick through each to swirl.

CHOCOLATE PAVLOVAS

SERVES 6

Use any combination of fruits in season.

1 tablespoon cocoa powder
1 tablespoon boiling water
3 egg whites
220 g (7 oz) caster (superfine) sugar
1 teaspoon vinegar
TOPPING
300 ml (10 fl oz/1¹/₄ cups) whipping cream
1 tablespoon chocolate spread
250 g (8 oz/1¹/₂ cups) mixed soft fruits, hulled
TO DECORATE
rose petals

1 Preheat oven to 140°C (275°F/Gas 1). Line 2 baking sheets with baking parchment.

2 Blend the cocoa with the boiling water.

3 Meanwhile, whisk the egg whites in a clean bowl until stiff. Gradually add the sugar, whisking well after each addition. Add the vinegar and whisk until the meringue is thick and forms soft peaks. Fold in the cocoa mixture, using a spatula.

4 Place 12 heaped spoonfuls of meringue well apart on the baking sheets. Bake for 45 minutes, then turn the oven off and leave the pavlovas in the oven until cool.

5 To make the topping, whisk the cream until thick, then carefully fold in the chocolate spread to give a marbled effect.

6 Spread the topping on 6 meringues and pile the fruit on top. Decorate with petals. Serve the remaining meringues separately.

LEFT: Chocolate pavlovas.

Chapter 2

ICES

— *and* —

ICED DRINKS

Frozen desserts and ice creams are great standbys to have in the freezer, and they are always a real treat. The ice creams featured here are all quick to make, and freeze within a few hours.

All have smooth, creamy textures, except the mint ice cream, which includes crunchy mint sticks. If you are storing ice creams long-term in the freezer, remember to transfer them to the refrigerator about an hour before serving to soften. *Frosted Lime Whip, Iced Chocolate Creams* and *Raspberry Ice Cream* can be frozen in their serving dishes and served straight from the freezer – or allowed to soften if you prefer.

Frothy iced chocolate milk shakes are great for children on a hot day; for a more sophisticated drink, try *Chocolate Velvet* or *Chocolate Fruit Frappé*.

TOP: Chocolate ice cream;
BOTTOM: Mint crisp ice cream.

CHOCOLATE ICE CREAM

SERVES 10

155 g (5 oz) plain (dark) chocolate, melted
400 g (14 oz) can condensed milk
550 ml (20 fl oz/2½ cups) double (thick) cream
TO DECORATE
chocolate curls or piped designs

1 Gradually add the condensed milk to the melted chocolate, stirring with a wooden spoon. Mix until evenly blended; some of the chocolate may set in small pieces.

2 Place the cream in a large bowl and whip until soft peaks form. Add the chocolate mixture and lightly fold into the cream, using a spatula, to yield a marbled mixture.

3 Pour into a plastic container, cover with a lid and place in the freezer for several hours until firm.

4 If the ice cream is stored for longer in a deep freeze, transfer to the refrigerator 1 hour before serving to soften.

5 Scoop the ice cream into balls and serve decorated with chocolate curls or piped designs.

MINT CRISP ICE CREAM

SERVES 8

Crushed mint sticks give this ice cream its crunchy texture. You can also try orange- or coffee-flavoured sticks.

115 ml (4 fl oz/½ cup) water
90 g (3 oz/1⅓ cup) caster (superfine) sugar
3 egg yolks
425 ml (15 fl oz/1¾ cups) whipping cream
120 g (3¾ oz) packet mint-flavoured chocolate
*   sticks, finely chopped*
TO DECORATE
chocolate cut-outs or curls

1 Bring the water to the boil in a small pan. Add the sugar and stir until completely dissolved, then boil rapidly for 1-2 minutes until the thread stage is reached. To test, press a small drop of the syrup between the backs of 2 teaspoons, then pull apart; a thread should form. If not, continue to boil and test again.

2 Place the egg yolks in a bowl and whisk, using an electric mixer. Pour in the syrup in a steady stream, whisking until pale, thick and cool.

3 In a separate bowl, whip the cream until soft peaks form. Lightly fold in the whisked mixture, using a spatula. Fold in the mint sticks.

4 Freeze in a covered plastic container until firm. If necessary, transfer to the refrigerator 1 hour before serving.

5 Scoop into small balls and serve decorated with chocolate cut-outs or curls.

CLEMENTINE SORBET

SERVES 6

6 clementines
300 ml (10 fl oz/1¼ cups) water
60 g (2 oz/¼ cup) caster (superfine) sugar
2 teaspoons powdered gelatine
90 g (3 oz) white chocolate, melted
2 egg whites
CHOCOLATE SAUCE
125 g (4 oz) plain (dark) chocolate
150 ml (5 fl oz/⅔ cup) single (light) cream
60 g (2 oz/2 tablespoons) golden syrup
15 g (¼ oz/3 teaspoons) butter

1 Pare the rind thinly from the clementines, place in a saucepan with the water and bring to the boil. Remove from the heat and stir in the sugar. Sprinkle on the gelatine, stirring until dissolved. Leave to cool.

2 Strain the clementine syrup into the chocolate, beating well until smooth.

3 Squeeze the juice from the clementines and stir into the chocolate mixture. Pour into a freezerproof container, cover and freeze for 2 hours until semi-frozen.

4 Whisk the egg whites in a clean bowl until stiff. Whisk the semi-frozen mixture in a separate bowl until smooth, then fold in the egg whites. Return to the container, cover and freeze until firm.

5 For the chocolate sauce, gently heat the ingredients in a small pan, stirring occasionally, until smooth. Cool.

6 Serve the sorbet with the chocolate sauce.

TOP: Clementine sorbet;
BOTTOM: Rich chocolate ice cream.

RICH CHOCOLATE ICE CREAM

SERVES 10

Ready-made custard — available in cartons — is used for speed. If you prefer, you can, of course, make your own, using custard powder.

155 g (5 oz) plain (dark) chocolate, melted
550 ml (20 fl oz/2¼ cups) ready-to-serve custard
300 ml (10 fl oz/1¼ cups) whipping cream
TO DECORATE
chocolate leaves or curls

1 Gradually stir the custard into the melted chocolate until smooth and evenly blended.

2 Whip the cream in a large mixing bowl until it is thick and forms soft peaks.

3 Using a spatula, fold the chocolate custard into the cream until evenly blended.

4 Pour the mixture into a plastic container, cover with a lid and freeze until firm.

5 If the ice cream is stored in the freezer for some time, transfer to the refrigerator 1 hour before serving.

6 Scoop into glass dishes and decorate with chocolate leaves or curls to serve.

ICED CHOCOLATE CREAMS

MAKES 8

Any liqueur or fruit juice can be used in place of the cherry brandy. To add a little texture, fold in some toasted chopped nuts before freezing.

125 g (4 oz) plain (dark) chocolate, melted
2 tablespoons cherry brandy
300 ml (10 fl oz/1¼ cups) whipping cream
2 egg whites
60 g (2 oz/¼ cup) caster (superfine) sugar
TO DECORATE
white chocolate flakes

1 Stir the cherry brandy and 4 tablespoons of the cream into the chocolate until smooth.

2 Place the remaining cream in a bowl and whip until thick.

3 Whisk the egg whites in a separate bowl, using clean beaters, until stiff. Gradually add the sugar, whisking well after each addition, until the meringue is stiff.

4 Lightly fold the meringue and chocolate mixture into the whipped cream, using a spatula, until the mixture is smooth and thick.

5 Spoon the mixture into 8 individual freezerproof dishes, cover and place in the freezer until required.

6 Serve frozen or partially thawed, topped with a few chocolate flakes.

FROSTED LIME WHIP

SERVES 6

thinly pared rind and juice of 4 limes
150 ml (5 fl oz/⅔ cup) water
185 g (6 oz/¾ cup) caster (superfine) sugar
2 teaspoons powdered gelatine
125 g (4 oz) white chocolate, melted
2 egg whites
TO DECORATE
lime twists and chocolate curls

1 Place the lime rind in a saucepan with the water and 125 g (4 oz/½ cup) of the sugar. Heat gently until the sugar has dissolved, then boil rapidly for 1 minute.

2 Soften the gelatine in 2 tablespoons water in a bowl. Strain the lime syrup into the bowl, stirring well until the gelatine has dissolved.

3 Add the syrup to the melted chocolate, stirring until smooth. Stir in the lime juice. Allow to cool, then cover and freeze until firm.

4 Whisk the egg whites in a clean bowl until stiff. Gradually add the remaining sugar, whisking well after each addition, until the meringue is thick.

5 Remove the lime mixture from the freezer and whisk until smooth. Lightly fold in the meringue mixture, using a spatula. Spoon the mixture into 6 individual freezerproof dishes and place in the freezer until required.

6 Decorate with lime twists and chocolate curls to serve.

TOP: Iced chocolate creams; BOTTOM: Frosted lime whip.

RASPBERRY ICE CREAM

SERVES 8

A smooth, creamy-textured ice cream with a tang of raspberries. Use other soft fruits, such as blackcurrants, if you prefer.

125 g (4 oz/³/₄ cup) raspberries
60 g (2 oz/¹/₃ cup) icing (confectioner's) sugar
155 g (5 oz) white chocolate, melted
300 ml (10 fl oz/1¹/₄ cups) whipping cream
TO DECORATE
raspberries
white chocolate leaves (optional)

1 Press the raspberries through a sieve into a bowl, to discard the seeds. Add the icing (confectioner's) sugar and stir until dissolved.

2 Add the raspberry mixture to the melted chocolate and beat with a wooden spoon until smooth.

3 Whip the cream in another bowl until thick. Lightly fold in the raspberry mixture, using a spatula, to give a smooth, thick, creamy mixture.

4 Place in a nylon piping bag fitted with a large star nozzle. Pipe a swirl of mixture into each of 8 individual freezerproof dishes. Freeze until firm.

5 To serve, decorate with raspberries, and chocolate leaves if you like.

NOTE
As an alternative, simply freeze the mixture in a covered plastic container and serve in scoops.

LAYERED CHOCOLATE ICE CREAM

SERVES 8

115 ml (4 fl oz/¹/₂ cup) water
90 g (3 oz/¹/₃ cup) caster (superfine) sugar
3 egg yolks
425 ml (15 fl oz/1³/₄ cups) double (thick) cream
90 g (3 oz) plain (dark) chocolate, melted
90 g (3 oz) white chocolate, melted

1 Bring the water to the boil in a small pan. Add the sugar and stir until completely dissolved, then boil rapidly for 1-2 minutes until the thread stage is reached. To test, press a small drop of the syrup between the backs of 2 teaspoons, then pull apart: a thread should form. If not, continue to boil and test.

2 Place the egg yolks in a bowl and whisk, using an electric mixer. Pour in the syrup in a steady stream, whisking until pale, thick and cool.

3 In a separate bowl, whip the cream until soft peaks form.

4 Stir half of the egg mixture into the melted plain (dark) chocolate. Stir the remainder into the melted white chocolate.

5 Fold half of the whipped cream into each mixture, using a spatula.

6 Pour the white ice cream into a 1 litre (1 3/4 pint) container, spreading it evenly. Pour the plain (dark) chocolate ice cream on top, smoothing the surface.

7 Cover and freeze for several hours until firm. Turn out and cut into slices to serve.

TOP: Raspberry ice cream; BOTTOM: Layered chocolate ice cream.

CHOCOLATE BOMBE

SERVES 8

2 eggs
60 g (2 oz/¼ cup) caster (superfine) sugar
60 g (2 oz/½ cup) plain (all purpose) flour,
    sifted
FILLING
300 ml (10 fl oz/1¼ cup) whipping cream
60 g (2 oz/½ cup) Amaretti biscuits (cookies),
    crushed
60 g (2 oz) white chocolate dots
30 g (1 oz/¼ cup) slivered almonds, toasted
10 maraschino cherries, chopped
250 g (8 oz) chocolate ice cream
TO DECORATE
icing (confectioner's) sugar for dusting
chocolate flakes

1 Preheat oven to 200°C (400°F/Gas 6). Line a
baking sheet with baking parchment and mark
on a 25 cm (10 in) circle. Invert the paper.

2 Whisk eggs and sugar in a heatproof bowl
over a pan of simmering water, until thick.
Remove and whisk until cool. Fold in flour.

3 Spread mixture over circle and bake for 5-8
minutes until firm. Cool on a wire rack and
dust with icing sugar. Cut into 12 wedges.

4 For the filling, whip the cream until thick.
Fold in the biscuits (cookies), chocolate dots,
almonds and cherries.

5 Line the base and sides of a 1.2 litre (2 pint)
pudding basin with eight of the sponge wedges.
Spread cream mixture in the basin, leaving a
hollow in the centre.

6 Fill with softened ice cream. Top with
remaining sponge and freeze until firm.

7 Turn out, dust with icing sugar and decorate
with chocolate flakes.

CHOCOLATE FRUIT ALASKAS

MAKES 4

Make a half quantity of chocolate sponge
drops (see page 53) or use thin slices of a
ready-made Swiss (jelly) roll for these. Any
soft fruit in season can be used.

4 chocolate sponge drops
125 g (4 oz/¾ cup) redcurrants
2 egg whites
125 g (4 oz/½ cup) caster (superfine) sugar
4 scoops chocolate ice cream
TO DECORATE
redcurrants
chocolate cut-outs (optional)

1 Place 4 sponge rounds well apart on a foil-
lined baking sheet.

2 Arrange the redcurrants in the centre of
each sponge round.

3 Whisk the egg whites in a clean bowl until
stiff. Gradually add the sugar, whisking well
after each addition, until the meringue is
thick. Place in a nylon piping bag fitted with a
star nozzle (tube).

4 Preheat grill to high and make sure that the
baking sheet will fit underneath with sufficient
space above.

5 Place a scoop of chocolate ice cream on top
of each fruit sponge and quickly spread or
pipe the meringue over to cover evenly.

6 Immediately place under the grill until the
meringue is lightly tinged brown.

7 Serve straight away, decorated with
redcurrants and chocolate cut-outs if you like.

TOP: Chocolate bombe; BOTTOM: Chocolate fruit alaskas.

ICED CHOCOLATE

SERVES 4

A refreshingly smooth drink on a hot summer's day. Make up a jug ready for use, and top with cream just before serving.

4 tablespoons drinking chocolate
550 ml (20 fl oz/2½ cups) milk
150 ml (5 fl oz/⅔ cup) whipping cream
short plain (dark) chocolate curls

1 Place the drinking chocolate and 150 ml (5 fl oz/⅔ cup) of the milk in a small saucepan. Bring to the boil, whisking constantly, then remove from the heat and leave until cold.

2 Meanwhile, chill the remaining milk and cream.

3 Place the cream in a bowl and whip until thick. Place 3 tablespoons in a nylon piping bag fitted with a star nozzle (tube).

4 Add the chilled milk and the chocolate mixture to the remaining cream and whisk until well blended.

5 Divide the chocolate mixture between 4 glasses and pipe a swirl of cream on top of each. Sprinkle with chocolate curls and serve, with straws.

CHOCOLATE MILK SHAKE

MAKES 2

Always popular with children; use milk chocolate for the sweeter version. Top with chocolate ice cream instead of vanilla if you prefer.

60 g (2 oz) plain (dark) or milk (semi-sweet)
  chocolate
450 ml (15 fl oz/1¾ cups) milk
250 g (8 oz) vanilla ice cream
TO DECORATE
cocoa powder for dusting

1 Heat the chocolate and 150 ml (5 fl oz/⅔ cup) of the milk in a small saucepan, stirring occasionally until melted. Remove from the heat and leave until cold.

2 Place the cooled chocolate mixture in a blender or food processor with the remaining milk and two-thirds of the ice cream. Blend or process until the mixture is smooth.

3 Pour into 2 tall glasses and top with the remaining ice cream. Dust with cocoa and serve, with straws.

FRONT: Iced chocolate; BACK: Chocolate milk shake.

CHOCOLATE VELVET

MAKES 4

A rich, dark drink flavoured with rum or brandy. Dilute to taste with soda water or lemonade. For a sweeter drink, use milk chocolate.

60 g (2 oz) plain (dark) or milk (semi-sweet) chocolate, melted
3 tablespoons dark rum or brandy
3 tablespoons thick Greek yogurt
2 teaspoons clear honey
lemonade or soda water to mix
TO DECORATE
chocolate flakes

1 Add the rum or brandy to the melted chocolate, stirring until smooth.

2 Add the yogurt and honey, stirring until thick and smooth. Divide the mixture between 4 tall glasses and fill with lemonade or soda water to taste. Stir to mix.

3 Sprinkle the top of each drink with chocolate flakes to serve.

CHOCOLATE FRUIT FRAPPE

MAKES 2

A refreshing drink with a tropical flavour. Try using melon, mango or banana instead of pineapple.

125 g (4 oz) fresh pineapple
60 g (2 oz) white chocolate, melted
1 tablespoon lime juice
1 teaspoon finely grated lime rind
60 g (2 oz) vanilla ice cream
lemonade or soda water to mix
TO DECORATE
lime twists
mint sprigs
pineapple wedges and leaves

1 Peel the pineapple, halve and remove the central core. Roughly chop the flesh and place in a blender or food processor. Work until smooth.

2 Add the chocolate, lime juice and rind, together with the ice cream. Blend for a few seconds until evenly mixed.

3 Pour the mixture into 2 tall glasses and fill up with lemonade or soda water. Stir gently to mix.

4 Spear lime twists, mint sprigs, pineapple wedges and leaves on to 2 cocktail (toothpick) sticks and use to decorate the drinks.

FRONT: Chocolate velvet;
BACK: Chocolate fruit frappé.

Chapter 3

CAKES, PASTRIES
and
GATEAUX

Baking cakes – even for a special occasion – needn't mean
spending hours in the kitchen. It's a good tip to keep
decorations simple and use ready-to-roll icing for
celebration cakes. The birthday cake, novelty clown and
festive cake are all simple to prepare. The other large
cakes included in this chapter combine moist textures with
contrasting flavours. Try the *Bounty Cake* with its creamy
coconut layer sandwiched between light chocolate sponge.
The small cake recipes feature soft sponges, light crisp and
nutty meringue mixtures, chocolate-topped choux buns
and crisp chocolate tarts filled with fruits in season.
Gâteaux are always a favourite, but they can be time-
consuming to prepare. Here you will find mouth-watering
recipes which you can make with the minimum of fuss. The
base of each gâteau can be made in advance and assembled
at the last minute.

FESTIVE CHOCOLATE CAKE

SERVES 12

A wonderful alternative to the traditional Christmas cake, with a festive feel.

60 g (2 oz/1/2 cup) glacé fruits, chopped
60 g (2 oz/1/2 cup) slivered almonds
90 g (3 oz) plain (dark) chocolate dots
30 g (1 oz/2 tablespoons) stem ginger, chopped
1 teaspoon finely grated orange rind
1 tablespoon orange juice
185 g (6 oz/1 1/2 cups) self-raising flour
185 g (6 oz/3/4 cup) caster (superfine) sugar
185 g (6 oz/3/4 cup) unsalted butter, softened
125 g (4 oz/1 1/4 cups) ground almonds
3 eggs
CHOCOLATE FUDGE ICING
125 g (4 oz) plain (dark) chocolate, in pieces
60 g (2 oz/1/4 cup) unsalted butter
1 egg
185 g (6 oz/1 cup) icing (confectioner's) sugar,
  sifted
TO DECORATE
marzipan holly leaves and berries (see note)

1 Preheat oven to 160°C (325°F/Gas 3). Grease and line a 20 cm (8 in) cake tin (pan) with baking parchment.

2 Place the glacé fruits, almonds, chocolate dots, ginger, orange rind and juice in a bowl. Stir until evenly mixed.

3 Place the remaining cake ingredients in another bowl and stir together with a wooden spoon. Beat for 2-3 minutes until smooth and glossy. Add the fruit mixture and stir until well mixed.

4 Transfer the cake mixture to the prepared tin and level the top. Bake for 1 1/4 hours, or until the cake springs back when lightly pressed in the centre. Leave the cake in the tin for 10 minutes, then turn out, remove the paper and cool on a wire rack.

5 For the chocolate fudge icing, place the chocolate and butter in a bowl over a saucepan of hot water and stir occasionally until melted. Stir in the egg, then beat in the icing sugar.

6 Place a plate underneath the wire rack. Pour the chocolate fudge icing over the cake, spreading it over the top and sides with a palette knife to cover evenly; allow the excess icing to fall on to the plate.

7 Gather the excess icing from the plate and place in a piping bag fitted with a star nozzle (tube). Pipe 8 swirls of icing around the top of the cake.

8 Arrange a pair of holly leaves on each swirl of icing with a few berries.

NOTE
To make marzipan holly leaves and berries, simply colour about 60 g (2 oz) marzipan green by kneading in a few drops of colouring. Roll out and cut out leaves using a holly-shaped cutter. Colour a tiny portion of marzipan red and mould tiny beads to resemble berries.

RIGHT: Festive chocolate cake.

BIRTHDAY CAKE

SERVES 10

Decorate to suit any occasion, with fresh or sugar-frosted flowers and matching ribbon; you will need about 1 m (1 yd).

185 g (6 oz/1½ cups) self-raising flour
185 g (6 oz/¾ cup) caster (superfine) sugar
185 g (6 oz/¾ cup) unsalted butter, softened
125 g (4 oz/1¼ cups) ground almonds
3 eggs
185 g (6 oz) mixed plain (dark), milk (semi-sweet) and white chocolate dots
TO DECORATE
375 g (12 oz) ready-to-roll icing
icing (confectioner's) sugar for dusting
2 tablespoons apricot jam, boiled and sieved

1 Preheat oven to 160°C (325°F/Gas 3). Grease and line a 20 cm (8 in) round cake tin (pan) with baking parchment.

2 Place all the cake ingredients, except the chocolate dots, in to a mixing bowl and beat together for 2-3 minutes until smooth and glossy. Stir in the chocolate dots.

3 Transfer to the prepared tin and level the top. Bake for 1¼ hours, or until the cake springs back when gently pressed in the centre. Turn out and cool on a wire rack.

4 Place the cake on a 20 cm (8 in) cake board. Roll out icing on a surface dusted with icing (confectioner's) sugar, to a 25 cm (10 in) round.

5 Brush the cake with apricot jam then cover with the icing, smoothing the top and side. Trim off excess icing at the base. Lightly crimp top edge and base of the cake if you wish.

6 Fit ribbon around side of cake and arrange flowers, tie with ribbon and place on top just before serving.

BOUNTY CAKE

SERVES 10

1 quantity all-in-one chocolate cake mixture (see page 47)
COCONUT LAYER
1 egg white
60 g (2 oz/¼ cup) caster (superfine) sugar
90 g (3 oz/1 cup) desiccated coconut
1 tablespoon cornflour (cornstarch)
TO DECORATE
1 quantity chocolate fudge icing (see page 42)
chocolate cut-outs
pared ribbons of fresh coconut

1 Preheat oven to 160°C (325°F/Gas 3). Grease and line an 18 cm (7 in) round cake tin (pan) with baking parchment.

2 For the coconut layer, whisk the egg white in a clean bowl until stiff. Gradually whisk in the sugar. Mix together the coconut and cornflour (cornstarch) and fold into the mixture.

3 Spread half of the cake mixture in the prepared tin. Spread the coconut layer on top and cover with the remaining cake mixture.

4 Bake for 1 hour, or until the cake springs back when lightly pressed in the centre. Turn out and cool on a wire rack.

5 Place a plate underneath the wire rack. Pour the chocolate fudge icing over the cake, spreading it over the top and sides with a palette knife to cover evenly; allow the excess icing to fall on to the plate.

6 Gather the excess icing from the plate and pipe a decorative border. Finish with chocolate cut-outs and coconut ribbons.

LEFT: Birthday cake.

COCOA CLOWN

SERVES 10

Children will love this easy cake — no fuss, just simple bold decoration!

ALL-IN-ONE CHOCOLATE CAKE
125 g (4 oz/1 cup) self-raising flour
1 tablespoon drinking chocolate or cocoa
    powder
1 teaspoon baking powder
125 g (4 oz/½ cup) caster (superfine) sugar
125 g (4 oz/½ cup) soft margarine
2 eggs
DECORATION
250 g (8 oz) chocolate-flavoured easy-to-roll
    icing
cocoa powder for dusting
2 tablespoons apricot jam, boiled and sieved
185 g (6 oz) white marzipan
red and green food colourings
icing (confectioner's) sugar for dusting

1 Preheat oven to 160°C (325°F/Gas 3). Grease and base line a 20 cm (8 in) sandwich tin (pan) with baking parchment.

2 Place all the cake ingredients in a mixing bowl. Beat together with a wooden spoon for 2-3 minutes until smooth and glossy.

3 Place the cake mixture in the prepared tin and level the top. Bake for 35-40 minutes, or until the cake springs back when gently pressed in the centre.

4 Loosen the edge of the cake with a palette knife, then turn out on to a wire rack and cool.

5 Roll out the chocolate icing on a surface lightly dusted with cocoa, to a 25 cm (10 in) round.

6 Brush the cake with apricot jam and carefully lift the icing on top of the cake. Smooth the top and sides and trim off the excess icing at the base. Mould 2 ears from the trimmings and press on to the sides of the cake.

7 Set aside two-thirds of the white marzipan. Colour two thirds of the remaining piece red and the other third green, by kneading in a few drops of each food colouring.

8 Shape a smiling mouth, a round nose and 7 small beads from the red marzipan.

9 Roll out the green marzipan on a surface lightly dusted with icing (confectioner's) sugar to a broad strip and cut out a bow tie shape. Press the red beads of marzipan on to it. Place the mouth, nose and bow tie in position.

10 Roll out a small piece of white marzipan, cut out 2 eye shapes and gently press into position.

11 Coarsely grate the remaining white marzipan for the hair. Position on each side of the face, securing with apricot jam.

12 Roll out thin strips of chocolate icing trimmings. Use to mark crosses on the eyes and lines around and on the mouth.

LEFT: Cocoa clown.

CHERRY ALMOND CAKE

SERVES 10

185 g (6 oz/³/₄ cup) soft light brown sugar
185 g (6 oz/³/₄ cup) unsalted butter, softened
185 g (6 oz/1¹/₃ cups) self-raising wholemeal
  flour
1 tablespoon cocoa powder
125 g (4 oz/1¹/₄ cups) ground almonds
3 eggs
90 g (3 oz/¹/₂ cup) glacé cherries, sliced
60 g (2 oz/¹/₃ cup) white chocolate dots
CHOCOLATE GLACÉ ICING
1 tablespoon cocoa powder
125 g (4 oz/³/₄ cup) icing (confectioner's) sugar
1 tablespoon boiling water
TO DECORATE
4 glacé cherries, halved
2 tablespoons white chocolate dots

1 Preheat oven to 160°C (325°F/Gas 3).
Grease and line an 18 cm (7 in) round cake tin
(pan) with baking parchment.

2 Place all the cake ingredients, except the
cherries and chocolate dots, in a mixing bowl.
Beat with a wooden spoon for 2-3 minutes until
smooth and glossy. Stir in the cherries and
chocolate dots.

3 Place the mixture in the prepared tin,
smooth top and bake for 1¹/₄ hours, or until the
cake springs back when lightly pressed in the
centre.

4 Turn out and cool on a wire rack.

5 Meanwhile make chocolate glacé icing. Sift
the cocoa and icing sugar into a bowl. Add the
boiling water and stir until smooth.

6 Spread icing on top of the cake and decorate
with cherries and chocolate dots.

CHOCOLATE GINGER CAKE

SERVES 10

185 g (6 oz/1¹/₂ cups) plain (all purpose) flour
60 g (2 oz/¹/₂ cup) medium oatmeal
1 egg
185 g (6 oz/¹/₂ cup) golden syrup
115 ml (4 fl oz/¹/₂ cup) milk
115 ml (4 fl oz/¹/₂ cup) vegetable oil
125 g (4 oz) plain (dark) chocolate, in pieces
90 g (3 oz/¹/₃ cup) caster (superfine) sugar
¹/₂ teaspoon bicarbonate of soda
30 g (1 oz/2 tablespoons) stem ginger
TO DECORATE
3 tablespoons chocolate spread
stem ginger slices

1 Preheat oven to 160°C (325°F/Gas 3).
Grease and line an 18 cm (7 in) square cake tin
(pan) with baking parchment. Place the flour,
oatmeal and egg in a mixing bowl.

2 Place the golden syrup, milk, oil, chocolate
and sugar in a saucepan. Heat gently, stirring
occasionally, until melted. Remove from the
heat, add the bicarbonate of soda and stir
well.

3 Add to the flour mixture and beat until
smooth. Stir in the ginger, then pour the
mixture into the prepared tin.

4 Bake for 1¹/₄ hours, or until the cake springs
back when lightly pressed in the centre. Cool
in the tin.

5 Warm the chocolate spread until liquid.
Turn out the cake and cover the top evenly
with the chocolate spread. Decorate with slices
of ginger.

TOP: Chocolate ginger cake; BOTTOM: Cherry almond cake.

CHOCOLATE & HAZELNUT FINGERS

MAKES 10

2 egg whites
125 g (4 oz/½ cup) caster (superfine) sugar
90 g (3 oz/¾ cup) ground almonds
1 tablespoon cocoa powder
1 tablespoon flaked almonds
FILLING
2 tablespoons chocolate hazelnut spread
4 tablespoons thick Greek yogurt
TO FINISH
icing (confectioner's) sugar for dusting

1 Preheat oven to 180°C (350°F/Gas 4). Line a baking sheet with baking parchment.

2 Whisk the egg whites in a clean bowl until stiff. Gradually add the sugar, whisking well after each addition, until stiff.

3 Mix together the ground almonds and cocoa thoroughly, then fold into the meringue, using a spatula, until evenly blended.

4 Transfer mixture to a nylon piping bag fitted with a 2 cm (¾ in) plain nozzle (tube) and pipe 20 fingers on to the baking sheet. Sprinkle flaked almonds on half of them.

5 Bake for 25-30 minutes until the fingers easily lift off the paper. Cool.

6 Place the chocolate hazelnut spread and yogurt in a bowl and carefully mix together using a spatula.

7 Sandwich the plain and almond topped fingers together in pairs with the filling. Dust with icing (confectioner's) sugar to serve.

FRUIT TARTLETS

MAKES 12

Use cherries, strawberries, raspberries, redcurrants, blueberries and grapes to fill these crisp chocolate cases.

125 g (4 oz/1 cup) plain (all purpose) flour
1 tablespoon cocoa powder
90 g (3 oz/⅓ cup) unsalted butter, in pieces
1 tablespoon caster (superfine) sugar
1 egg yolk
1-2 tablespoons water
FILLING
6 tablespoons apricot jam, boiled and sieved
115 ml (4 fl oz/½ cup) whipping cream, whipped
250 g (8 oz/1½ cups) mixed soft fruits

1 Preheat oven to 200°C (400°F/Gas 6). Lightly flour 12 individual tartlet tins (pans) and place on a baking sheet.

2 Sift flour and cocoa into a mixing bowl. Rub in the butter until the mixture resembles fine breadcrumbs. Stir in the sugar.

3 Stir in the egg yolk and enough water to mix to form a firm dough.

4 Roll out thinly on a lightly floured surface and cut out 12 rounds; use to line the tartlet tins (pans). Prick the bases with a fork, chill for 5 minutes, then bake for 10-12 minutes until the pastry edges are crisp. Cool in the tins.

5 Brush each pastry case with apricot jam, add a spoonful of cream and fill with an arrangement of prepared fruits. Glaze the fruit with a little apricot jam. Serve immediately.

TOP & BOTTOM: Chocolate & hazelnut fingers; CENTRE: Fruit tartlets.

CHOCOLATE SPONGE DROPS

MAKES 10

2 eggs
60 g (2 oz/¹⁄₄ cup) caster (superfine) sugar
60 g (2 oz/¹⁄₂ cup) less 2 teaspoons plain (all purpose) flour
2 teaspoons cocoa powder
FILLING & TOPPING
150 ml (5 fl oz/²⁄₃ cup) whipping cream
3 tablespoons chocolate spread
1 tablespoon plain (dark) chocolate dots
icing (confectioner's) sugar for dusting

1 Preheat oven to 200°C (400°F/Gas 6). Line 2 baking sheets with baking parchment.

2 Place the eggs and sugar in a heatproof bowl over a saucepan of simmering water. Whisk until the mixture is thick and pale. Remove bowl from pan and whisk until the mixture leaves a trail when the beaters are lifted.

3 Sift the flour and cocoa together on to the surface of the whisked mixture, then fold in carefully using a spatula.

4 Drop 10 spoonfuls of the mixture, spaced apart, on to each baking sheet and bake for 5-8 minutes until firm to touch. Cool on the baking sheets.

5 Whip the cream until thick and fold in 1 tablespoon chocolate spread.

6 Warm the remaining chocolate spread in a small saucepan until liquid, then spread evenly over the tops of 10 of the sponge drops.

7 Sandwich the plain and coated sponges together with cream. Top with cream and chocolate dots. Dust with icing (confectioner's) sugar.

TRUFFLE CAKES

MAKES 10

A great way to use up leftover chocolate combined with crushed biscuits (cookies) and cake crumbs.

125 g (4 oz/2 cups) plain cake, crumbled
60 g (2 oz/¹⁄₃ cup) raisins
60 g (2 oz/¹⁄₂ cup) pine nuts
30 g (1 oz/¹⁄₄ cup) ratafias or macaroons, crushed
1 teaspoon finely grated orange rind
3 tablespoons orange juice
185 g (6 oz) milk (semi-sweet) chocolate, melted
TO FINISH
125 g (4 oz) milk (semi-sweet) or white chocolate, grated

1 In a bowl, mix together the cake crumbs, raisins, pine nuts, ratafias or macaroons, orange rind and juice until thoroughly blended.

2 Add three quarters of the melted chocolate and stir until the mixture begins to bind together.

3 Take a heaped spoonful of mixture and shape into a neat ball. Repeat to make 10 truffles in total.

4 Pour the remaining melted chocolate on to a piece of baking parchment. Roll each ball of mixture in the melted chocolate to cover thinly, then coat with grated chocolate. Leave to set.

TOP: Chocolate sponge drops; BOTTOM: Truffle cakes.

CHOCOLATE MERINGUES

MAKES 8

Meringues can be made in advance and stored in a tin until you need them. Topped with flavoured cream and fruit, they look most attractive.

2 egg whites
125 g (4 oz/¹/₂ cup) caster (superfine) sugar
FILLING
150 ml (5 fl oz/²/₃ cup) double (thick) cream
1 tablespoon chocolate hazelnut spread
125 g (4 oz) strawberries, sliced

1 Preheat oven to 110°C (225°F/Gas ¹/₄). Line a baking sheet with baking parchment.

2 Whisk the egg whites in a clean bowl until stiff. Gradually add the sugar, whisking well after each addition, until stiff.

3 Using 2 tablespoons, shape the meringue into 8 ovals, placing them on the baking sheet.

4 Bake for about 1 hour, or until the meringues easily lift off the paper. Leave to cool.

5 Whip the cream and chocolate hazelnut spread together in a bowl until thick. Place in a nylon piping bag fitted with a star nozzle (tube).

6 Pipe chocolate cream shells on each meringue and arrange the strawberry slices on top.

CHOCOLATE CHOUX BUNS

MAKES 12

CHOUX PASTRY
60 g (2 oz/¹/₄ cup) butter
150 ml (5 fl oz/²/₃ cup) water
75 g (2¹/₂ oz/¹/₂ cup) plain (all purpose) flour
2 eggs
FILLING AND TOPPING
125 g (4 oz) plain (dark) or white chocolate
300 ml (10 fl oz/1¹/₄ cups) whipping cream

1 Preheat oven to 200°C (400°F/Gas 6). Lightly flour a baking sheet.

2 Heat the butter and water in a saucepan until melted. Bring to the boil, remove from the heat and beat in the flour all at once to form a soft paste. Cook, stirring for 30 seconds, until the paste forms a ball. Remove from the heat.

3 Add the eggs one at a time, beating well after each addition.

4 Spoon the mixture into 12 balls on the baking sheet, spacing well apart. Bake for 20-25 minutes until well risen and golden brown. Slit each choux bun and transfer to a wire cooling rack.

5 Meanwhile melt chocolate, stirring occasionally, until smooth.

6 Whip the cream until thick. Open each choux bun and fill with cream. Dip tops into chocolate to coat evenly. Leave to set.

TOP & BOTTOM: Chocolate choux buns; CENTRE: Chocolate meringues.

REDCURRANT MERINGUE GATEAU

SERVES 10

A sumptuous gâteau for a special occasion, which is far quicker to make than it looks. Use any soft fruits which are in season.

MERINGUE
3 egg whites
¼ teaspoon cream of tartar
185 g (6 oz/¾ cup) caster (superfine) sugar
60 g (2 oz) plain (dark) chocolate, grated
FILLING
300 ml (10 fl oz/1¼ cups) whipping cream
2 tablespoons chocolate spread
250 g (8 oz) redcurrants
TO DECORATE
sprigs of redcurrants
chocolate leaves (optional)

1 Preheat oven to 110°C (225°F/Gas ¼). Line a large baking sheet with baking parchment and draw on three 18 cm (7 in) circles. Invert the paper.

2 Place the egg whites and cream of tartar in a clean bowl and whisk until stiff. Gradually add the sugar, whisking well after each addition, until the mixture is thick and stands up in soft peaks.

3 Add the grated chocolate and carefully fold in, using a spatula, until evenly blended.

4 Divide the chocolate meringue between the 3 marked circles and spread evenly to the edges.

5 Bake in the centre of the oven for about 1 hour, or until the meringue rounds easily lift off the paper. Transfer to a wire rack and allow to cool.

6 To make the filling, whip the cream in a clean bowl until thick. Add the chocolate spread and fold in carefully until evenly blended.

7 Place 3 tablespoons of chocolate cream in a nylon piping bag fitted with a star nozzle (tube). Use the remaining cream to cover the

LEFT: Redcurrant meringue gâteau.

tops of two meringue layers.

8 Arrange the redcurrants over the cream and stack the meringue-filled layers together on a serving plate. Position the plain meringue layer on top.

9 To decorate, pipe cream swirls around the edge and arrange the redcurrant sprigs on top. Add chocolate leaves too, if desired. Serve immediately.

CHESTNUT & BLUEBERRY SLICE

SERVES 10

375 g (12 oz) cooking apples
1 tablespoon caster (superfine) sugar
480 g (1 lb) can unsweetened chestnut purée
125 g (4 oz) milk (semi-sweet) chocolate,
  melted
24 sponge fingers
3 tablespoons orange juice or sherry
185 g (6 oz) blueberries
60 g (2 oz) plain (dark) chocolate, grated
TO DECORATE
blueberries

1 Peel, core and slice the apples into a small saucepan. Add 1 tablespoon water and the sugar. Cook until the apples are pulpy. Place in a food processor with the chestnut purée and melted chocolate; work until smooth. Leave to cool.

2 Dip 8 sponge fingers into the orange juice or sherry and arrange on an oblong serving dish. Spread with a quarter of the chocolate filling and cover with half of the blueberries.

3 Repeat these layers, finishing with the remaining dipped sponge fingers.

4 Spread the top and sides of the gâteau with all but 3 tablespoons of the remaining chocolate mixture. Coat the sides with grated chocolate.

5 Pipe a decorative chocolate border on top of the gâteau and decorate with blueberries.

LEMON CHEESE GATEAU

SERVES 10

3 lemons
250 g (8 oz) skimmed milk soft cheese
150 ml (5 fl oz/²/₃ cup) thick Greek yogurt
185 g (6 oz) white chocolate, melted
1 1/2 packets (12) trifle sponges
TOPPING
300 ml (10 fl oz/1¼ cups) whipping cream
60 g (2 oz) white chocolate, grated
TO DECORATE
1 lemon slice, cut into triangles
lemon geranium leaves

1 Finely grate the lemon rind from two of the lemons and squeeze the juice from all 3 lemons.

2 Place the soft cheese and yogurt in a mixing bowl and beat together until smooth. Stir in the lemon rind and 2 tablespoons of the lemon juice.

3 Gradually add the lemon mixture to the melted chocolate, stirring until smooth.

4 Cut each trifle sponge into 3 slices. Line the base of a 20 cm (8 in) springform cake tin (pan) with plastic food wrap. Use half of the sponge slices – quickly dipped into lemon juice – to line the base and halfway up the side of the tin.

5 Spread half of the lemon mixture on top and cover with another layer of lemon-dipped sponge slices. Repeat with remaining lemon mixture and lemon-dipped sponge slices.

6 Cover the surface and chill over night or for 2 hours until firm.

7 Meanwhile make the topping. Whip the cream in a clean bowl until thick. Place 4 tablespoons in a piping bag fitted with a star nozzle (tube).

8 Release the cake tin (pan), uncover the surface and carefully invert the cake on to a plate. Remove food wrap. Spread whipped cream over the top and side of the gâteau using a palette knife. Press white chocolate on to the side of the gâteau to cover evenly.

9 Pipe a cream border around the top and decorate with lemon triangles and geranium leaves to serve.

LEFT: Lemon cheese gâteau.

CHOCOLATE GATEAU

SERVES 12

3 tablespoons marsala or brandy
60 g (2 oz/¹/₃ cup) raisins
125 g (4 oz/¹/₂ cup) unsalted butter
185 g (6 oz) plain (dark) chocolate, in pieces
3 eggs, separated
125 g (4 oz/¹/₂ cup) caster (superfine) sugar
90 g (3 oz/³/₄ cup) self-raising flour, sifted
60 g (2 oz/¹/₂ cup) ground almonds
FILLING & TOPPING
185 g (6 oz) plain (dark) chocolate
300 ml (10 fl oz/1¼ cups) whipping cream
4 tablespoons morello cherry jam
chocolate cut-outs

1 Preheat oven to 180°C (350°F/Gas 4). Grease and line a 20 cm (8 in) round cake tin (pan) with parchment paper.

2 Warm the marsala and raisins together, take off the heat, and stir in the butter and chocolate until melted and smooth.

3 Whisk the egg yolks and sugar in a heat-proof bowl over a pan of simmering water until thick and pale. Remove the bowl from the heat. Stir in the chocolate mixture, then fold in the flour and ground almonds. Fold in the stiffly whisked egg whites.

4 Pour into the prepared cake tin (pan) and bake for 40-45 minutes. Turn out, remove the paper and cool on a wire rack.

5 For the filling and topping, heat the chocolate with half of the cream until melted; cool until thick.

6 Whip remaining cream. Halve cake and sandwich with jam and half the cream.

7 Cover cake with chocolate cream; stir excess into remaining whipped cream and use to pipe a border. Top with chocolate cut-outs.

TIPSY MOCHA GATEAU

SERVES 12

A plain, extra moist gâteau soaked in mocha syrup. You can flavour the syrup with lime, lemon or orange juice rather than coffee if you prefer.

CAKE MIXTURE
185 g (6 oz/1½ cups) self-raising flour
1½ teaspoons baking powder
1 tablespoon cocoa powder
185 g (6 oz/¾ cup) caster (superfine) sugar
185 g (6 oz/¾ cup) soft margarine
3 eggs
MOCHA SYRUP & ICING
300 ml (10 fl oz/1¼ cups) water
250 g (8 oz/1¼ cups) caster (superfine) sugar
2 teaspoons instant coffee granules
3 tablespoons chocolate cream liqueur
125 g (4 oz) plain (dark) chocolate
TO DECORATE
30 g (1 oz) white chocolate, melted
300 ml (10 fl oz/1¼ cups) whipping cream
*   (optional)*

1 Preheat oven to 160°C (325°F/Gas 3). Grease and base line a 23 cm (9 in) springform cake tin (pan) with baking parchment.

2 Sift the flour, baking powder and cocoa into a mixing bowl. Add the sugar, margarine and eggs and mix together with a wooden spoon. Beat for 2-3 minutes until smooth and glossy.

3 Transfer the mixture to the prepared tin (pan), smooth the top and bake for 40-50 minutes, or until the cake springs back when lightly pressed in the centre.

4 Loosen the edge with a palette knife, release the tin and transfer the cake to a wire rack.

5 To make the mocha syrup, bring the water to the boil in a medium saucepan. Stir in the sugar and coffee until dissolved. Return to the boil and boil the syrup for 3-4 minutes until it measures 300 ml (10 fl oz/1¼ cups).

6 Transfer half of the syrup to a jug and stir in the chocolate cream liqueur.

7 Add the plain (dark) chocolate, in pieces, to the remaining syrup in the pan and stir occasionally until melted. Leave until thick.

8 Return the cake to the clean cake tin (pan) and pour the liqueur-flavoured syrup over the surface. Release the tin (pan) and transfer the cake, on the cake tin (pan) base, to a wire rack over a plate. Pour the thickened chocolate icing over the cake, spreading it evenly to cover.

9 Place the white chocolate in a greaseproof (waxed) paper piping bag, snip off the end and pipe parallel white chocolate lines on top of the gâteau. Draw a cocktail (toothpick) stick across the lines in one direction to create a feathered design.

10 When the icing has set, lift the cake off the base and transfer to a plate. Serve with whipped cream, if desired.

RIGHT: Tipsy mocha gâteau.

CHOCOLATE ROULADE

SERVES 8

5 eggs, separated
155 g (5 oz/²/₃ cup) caster (superfine) sugar
3 tablespoons hot water
30 g (1 oz/¹/₄ cup) ground almonds
185 g (6 oz) plain (dark) chocolate, melted
FILLING
150 ml (5 fl oz/²/₃ cup) whipping cream
1 tablespoon rose water
TO DECORATE
chocolate leaves
chocolate roses (optional)

1 Preheat oven to 200°C (400°F/Gas 6).
Grease and line a 33 x 23 cm (13 x 9 in) Swiss
(jelly) roll tin (pan) with baking parchment.

2 Whisk the egg yolks and sugar in a
heatproof bowl over a pan of simmering water
until thick and pale. Fold in the water, ground
almonds and chocolate.

3 Whisk the egg whites with clean beaters in a
clean bowl until stiff, fold into the mixture.

4 Pour into the prepared tin and bake for 15-
20 minutes or until the cake springs back when
lightly pressed in the centre. Cool in the tin,
covered with a damp tea towel.

5 In a bowl, whip the cream with the rose
water until thick.

6 Turn the cake out on to a piece of baking
parchment dusted with icing (confectioner's)
sugar. Trim all the edges, spread all but 3
tablespoons cream over the cake. Then roll up
from a short edge into a neat roll.

7 Decorate with reserved cream and chocolate
leaves. Add tiny roses too, if desired.

CHOCOLATE CHEESECAKE

SERVES 10

BASE
185 g (6 oz/1²/₃ cups) digestive biscuits
    (cookies), crushed
60 g (2 oz/¹/₄ cup) unsalted butter, melted
FILLING
375 g (12 oz) cream cheese
175 ml (6 fl oz/³/₄ cup) single (light) cream
185 g (6 oz) milk (semi-sweet) chocolate,
    melted
1 tablespoon orange juice
TOPPING
2 tablespoons chocolate spread, warmed
90 g (3 oz) white chocolate curls
cocoa powder for dusting

1 Mix together the crushed biscuits (cookies)
and butter and press evenly over the base of a
20 cm (8 in) springform cake tin (pan).

2 Beat together the cream cheese and cream
with a wooden spoon until smooth.

3 Add the orange juice to the melted
chocolate, then gradually stir in the cream
cheese mixture until evenly blended.

4 Quickly spread the mixture evenly over the
biscuit (cookie) base in the tin. Chill until set.

5 Release the tin and carefully transfer the
cheesecake to a plate. Spread the top with
chocolate spread and cover with white
chocolate curls.

6 Lay 4 strips of greaseproof (waxed) paper
with spaces in between on the cheesecake and
dust the top with cocoa. Carefully remove the
paper strips to reveal the pattern.

TOP: Chocolate cheesecake; BOTTOM: Chocolate roulade.

Chapter 4

BISCUITS
— *and* —
COOKIES

No-bake recipes mean no fuss, little effort and plenty of rewards. This chapter has quick recipes using melted chocolate to set interesting mixtures of ingredients together. Simply chill, cut and serve. These make wonderful standby nibbles for lunch boxes or picnics and children love them.

Favourite bakes — like *Shortbread* and *Flapjacks* — are made extra special with the addition of chocolate. Smarter biscuits (cookies) include *Florentines*, and *Brandy Snaps* that can be filled with chocolate cream. Elegant, crisp *Chocolate Russe Biscuits (Cookies)* are the perfect complement to ice creams and whipped or creamy desserts. If you have time, mould *Brandy Snaps* or *Russe Biscuits (Cookies)* over lightly oiled oranges to make basket shapes — ideal containers for scoops of ice cream.

FLORENTINES

MAKES 18

60 g (2 oz/¹/₄ cup) unsalted butter
90 g (3 oz/¹/₃ cup) caster (superfine) sugar
3 tablespoons thick Greek yogurt
60 g (2 oz/¹/₂ cup) slivered almonds
30 g (1 oz/¹/₄ cup) toasted hazelnuts, chopped
30 g (1 oz/¹/₄ cup) pine nuts
30 g (1 oz/2 tablespoons) glacé cherries
30 g (1 oz/2 tablespoons) cut mixed peel
30 g (1 oz/2 tablespoons) angelica, chopped
1 1/2 tablespoons plain (all purpose) flour
TO DECORATE
185 g (6 oz) milk (semi-sweet) or white
  chocolate, melted

1 Preheat oven to 190°C (375°F/Gas 5). Line 2 baking sheets with baking parchment.

2 Gently heat the butter, sugar and yogurt in a pan, stirring occasionally, until melted.

3 Remove from the heat and stir in the nuts, cherries, peel and angelica. Stir in the flour until evenly mixed.

4 Place 5 heaped teaspoonfuls of mixture, spaced well apart, on each baking sheet. Bake for 4-5 minutes until pale golden. Leave on the paper until firm, then cool on a wire rack. Repeat to make about 18 florentines.

5 To decorate, spread the melted chocolate thinly on a large piece of baking parchment. Place the florentines on the chocolate and chill for 2 minutes. Peel the paper away and separate the florentines.

CHOCOLATE RUSSE COOKIES

MAKES 18

These biscuits – shaped into thin tubes – are delicious with ice creams and creamy desserts.

1 egg white
60 g (2 oz/¹/₄ cup) caster (superfine) sugar
30 g (1 oz/¹/₄ cup) plain (all purpose) flour
2 teaspoons cocoa powder
30 g (1 oz/6 teaspoons) unsalted butter, melted
TO DECORATE
30 g (1 oz) white chocolate, melted

1 Preheat oven to 200°C (400°F/Gas 6). Line 2 baking sheets with baking parchment.

2 Whisk the egg white in a clean bowl until stiff. Gradually add the sugar, whisking well after each addition.

3 Sift the flour and cocoa over the mixture, add the melted butter and whisk gently until well blended.

4 Place 4 teaspoonfuls of the mixture, spaced well apart, on each baking sheet. Spread each thinly to a 10 cm (4 in) square.

5 Bake, one tray at a time, for 3-4 minutes until firm at the edges. Loosen each square and quickly roll into a thin tube around a wooden spoon handle. Cool on a wire rack.

6 Repeat this procedure to make 18 biscuits. Using a greaseproof (waxed) paper piping bag, drizzle the biscuits with melted white chocolate.

TOP: Chocolate russe cookies; BOTTOM: Florentines.

CHOCOLATE SHORTBREAD

SERVES 10

This oat-textured shortbread may be flavoured with 1 teaspoon grated citrus rind if you prefer.

140 g (5 oz/1¼ cups) plain (all purpose) flour
30 g (1 oz/2 tablespoons) medium oatmeal
60 g (2 oz/¼ cup) caster (superfine) sugar
125 g (4 oz/½ cup) unsalted butter
TOPPING
90 g (3 oz) white chocolate, melted
30 g (1 oz) plain (dark) chocolate, melted

1 Preheat oven to 160°C (325°F/Gas 3). Grease and line the base of a 20 cm (8 in) sandwich tin (pan) with baking parchment.

2 Sift the flour into a bowl. Stir in the oatmeal and sugar. Add the butter in small pieces and rub in using the fingertips until the mixture begins to bind together.

3 Spread the mixture evenly over the base of the prepared tin and press down to level.

4 Bake for 25-30 minutes until pale in colour. Cool in the tin, then turn out and remove the paper. Leave on a wire rack until cold.

5 Spread the white chocolate evenly over the top of the shortbread. Using a greaseproof (waxed) paper piping bag, pipe lines of plain (dark) chocolate at 2.5 cm (1 in) intervals across the white chocolate. Draw a cocktail (toothpick) stick across the lines of chocolate to give a feathered effect. Leave to set, then cut into wedges.

CHOCOLATE BRANDY SNAPS

MAKES 24

Serve these filled with chocolate cream, or plain with ice cream.

60 g (2 oz/¼ cup) unsalted butter
60 g (2 oz/¼ cup) caster (superfine) sugar
60 g (2 oz/2 tablespoons) clear honey
30 g (1 oz) plain (dark) chocolate
2 teaspoons brandy
60 g (2 oz/½ cup) plain (all purpose) flour
FILLING
300 ml (10 fl oz/1¼ cups) whipping cream
60 g (2 oz) plain (dark) chocolate, melted

1 Preheat oven to 200°C (400°F/Gas 6). Lightly butter 2 baking sheets.

2 Gently heat the butter, sugar, honey and chocolate, stirring occasionally, until melted. Remove from the heat and stir in the brandy and flour.

3 Place 4 teaspoonfuls of the mixture, spaced well apart on each baking sheet. Bake, one sheet at a time, for 3-4 minutes until brown.

4 Allow to cool for 1 minute, then quickly roll each brandy snap loosely around a wooden spoon handle. When firm, slide off and cool on a wire rack. Repeat to make 24.

5 To make the filling, stir 2 tablespoons of the cream into the melted chocolate. Whip remaining cream until thick, then fold in the chocolate. Pipe chocolate cream into each brandy snap to fill.

TOP: Chocolate shortbread; BOTTOM: Chocolate brandy snaps.

CHOCOLATE CARAMEL BARS

MAKES 16

Use any crushed biscuits (cookies) for the base of these caramel bars, and add nuts and dried fruit to the filling if you wish.

90 g (3 oz/¹/₃ cup) unsalted butter
185 g (6 oz/1²/₃ cups) digestive biscuits
 (cookies), crushed
3 x 100 g (3¹/₂ oz) bars of creamy toffee
3 tablespoons water
125 g (4 oz) plain (dark) chocolate, melted
30 g (1 oz) white chocolate, melted

1 Line the base and sides of a 28 x 18 cm (11 x 7 in) Swiss (jelly) roll tin (pan) with baking parchment.

2 Melt the butter in a small pan, remove from the heat and stir in the crushed biscuits (cookies) until evenly blended. Press the biscuit (cookie) mixture evenly over the base of the tin until level.

3 Heat the toffee and water in a small saucepan, stirring occasionally, until melted. Pour evenly over the biscuit (cookie) base. Allow to cool.

4 Spread the plain chocolate evenly over the caramel layer, smoothing with a palette knife. Using a greaseproof (waxed) paper piping bag, drizzle the white chocolate over the top.

5 When set, cut into bars.

CHOCOLATE BISCUIT (COOKIE) CRUNCH

SERVES 12

Use plain — not too sweet — biscuits (cookies) for this chocolate crunch. Vary the nuts, if you like, and try using crème de menthe cherries.

125 g (4 oz) plain (dark) chocolate
60 g (2 oz/¹/₄ cup) unsalted butter
60 g (2 oz/2 tablespoons) golden syrup
220 g (7 oz) Petit Beurre biscuits (cookies)
60 g (2 oz/1 cup) toasted hazelnuts
60 g (2 oz/¹/₃ cup) maraschino cocktail cherries
TO DECORATE
90 g (3 oz) plain (dark) chocolate, melted
4 cherries, sliced
12 whole hazelnuts

1 Grease and line the base of a 20 cm (8 in) sandwich tin (pan) with baking parchment.

2 Gently heat the chocolate, butter and syrup, stirring occasionally, until melted.

3 Meanwhile, lightly crush the biscuits and roughly chop the nuts and cherries.

4 Add the biscuits (cookies) and nuts to the syrup mixture, stirring until well coated. Stir in the cherries. Spread over the base of the prepared tin (pan) and press down firmly to level.

5 Spread the melted chocolate evenly over the top of the mixture and decorate with cherry slices and hazelnuts. Leave to set.

6 Loosen the edge of the mixture with a palette knife, turn out and remove the paper. Cut into wedges to serve.

TOP: Chocolate caramel bars; BOTTOM: Chocolate biscuit (cookie) crunch.

CHOCOLATE FLAPJACKS

MAKES 16

To vary this favourite ultra-quick recipe, add raisins, cherries or mixed peel, or replace the coconut with chopped nuts.

4 tablespoons clear honey
60 g (2 oz/¼ cup) unsalted butter
60 g (2 oz/¼ cup) soft light brown sugar
60 g (2 oz) plain (dark) chocolate
60 g (2 oz/⅓ cup) glacé cherries
155 g (5 oz/1¾ cups) rolled oats
30 g (1 oz/⅓ cup) desiccated coconut
TO DECORATE
icing (confectioner's) sugar for dusting

1 Preheat oven to 190°C (375°F/Gas 5). Line an 18 cm (7 in) shallow square tin (pan) with baking parchment.

2 Gently heat the honey, butter, sugar and chocolate, stirring occasionally, until melted. Remove from the heat and stir in the cherries, oats and coconut until thoroughly blended. Spread the mixture evenly in the prepared tin (pan).

3 Bake for 25-30 minutes, or until the mixture feels firm.

4 Cool in the tin (pan), then turn out, remove the paper and cut into squares. Dust with icing (confectioner's) sugar to serve.

CHOCOLATE MUESLI BARS

MAKES 16

These quick, healthy bars are great for lunch boxes. Use any combination of dried fruits and nuts.

125 g (4 oz) white chocolate
3 tablespoons clear honey
30 g (1 oz/2 tablespoons) peanut kernels
60 g (2 oz/⅓ cup) jumbo oats
2 tablespoons sesame seeds
60 g (2 oz/⅓ cup) raisins
60 g (2 oz/½ cup) dried apricots, chopped
60 g (2 oz/⅓ cup) natural wheat mini flakes
TO DECORATE
30 g (1 oz) plain (dark) chocolate, melted

1 Line an 18 cm (7 in) shallow square tin (pan) with baking parchment.

2 Gently heat the white chocolate with the honey, stirring occasionally, until melted.

3 Meanwhile toast the peanuts and oats on a baking sheet under a hot grill until golden brown.

4 Add to the chocolate mixture with the sesame seeds, raisins, apricots and wheat flakes; stir until thoroughly mixed.

5 Spread the mixture evenly in the prepared tin (pan) and leave for a few minutes to set.

6 Turn out and remove the paper. Using a greaseproof (waxed) paper piping bag, drizzle the plain chocolate over the top of the muesli mixture and leave to set. Cut into bars.

TOP: Chocolate flapjacks; BOTTOM: Chocolate muesli bars.

CHOCOLATE DOT COOKIES

MAKES 28

125 g (4 oz/½ cup) unsalted butter, softened
125 g (4 oz/½ cup) light soft brown sugar
2 tablespoons milk
185 g (6 oz/1⅓ cups) self-raising wholemeal
    flour
90 g (3 oz) plain (dark) chocolate dots
TO DECORATE
cocoa powder or melted plain (dark)
    chocolate

1 Preheat oven to 150°C (300°F/Gas 2). Line 2 baking sheets with baking parchment.

2 Place the butter and sugar in a mixing bowl. Beat together with a wooden spoon until light and fluffy.

3 Add the milk, flour and chocolate dots and fold in, using a spatula, to form a soft dough.

4 Shape the mixture into 28 round walnut-sized pieces and place them well apart on the baking sheets.

5 Flatten each ball of dough with the fingers and bake for 15-20 minutes until the biscuits (cookies) are flat and lightly browned at the edges.

6 Cool on the baking sheets and dust with cocoa powder or drizzle with melted plain (dark) chocolate to serve.

CHOCOLATE CLUSTERS

MAKES 12

A great favourite with children. Use any cereal which comes to hand, plus a mixture of dried fruits and nuts.

90 g (3 oz/1⅓ cup) unsalted butter
4 tablespoons clear honey
4 tablespoons drinking chocolate
100 g (3½ oz/⅔ cup) natural wheat mini flakes
60 g (2 oz/1⅓ cup) sultanas
TO DECORATE
white chocolate curls

1 Arrange 12 paper cases on a baking sheet.

2 Heat the butter, honey and drinking chocolate in a saucepan, stirring occasionally, until melted.

3 Remove from the heat and add the wheat flakes and sultanas, stirring until well coated.

4 Divide the mixture evenly between the paper cases and decorate with white chocolate curls.

TOP & BOTTOM: Chocolate dot cookies; CENTRE: Chocolate clusters.

COCO TOFFEE BITES

MAKES 16

Children's favourite cereal made into quick chocolate treats. Serve plain or dipped into white chocolate and sprinkled with fruit rind.

100 g (3½ oz) bar creamy toffee
60 g (2 oz) milk (semi-sweet) chocolate
1 tablespoon orange juice
90 g (3 oz/2 cups) chocolate flavoured rice
  cereal
60 g (2 oz) white chocolate, melted
1 teaspoon grated orange rind

1 Grease and line the base of an 18 cm (7 in) shallow square tin (pan) with baking parchment.

2 Gently heat the toffee, chocolate and orange juice in a saucepan, stirring occasionally, until melted and smooth.

3 Remove from the heat, add the cereal and stir until evenly coated.

4 Spread the mixture in the prepared tin (pan) and press down firmly to level. Leave to set.

5 Turn out of the tin (pan), remove the paper and cut into 16 bars. Dip the end of each bar into the melted white chocolate and sprinkle with orange rind. Leave to set.

CHOCOLATE CORN CUPS

MAKES 12

Pop your own corn, or buy it ready-popped without any flavouring. Use white, milk (semi-sweet) or plain (dark) chocolate and any mixture of fruits.

2 tablespoons corn oil
30 g (1 oz/2 tablespoons) popping corn
125 g (4 oz) plain (dark) chocolate, melted
2 tablespoons sesame seeds
4 dried dates, chopped
30 g (1 oz/½ cup) dried apple slices, chopped
TO DECORATE
grated milk (semi-sweet) or plain (dark)
  chocolate curls

1 Arrange 12 paper cake cases on a baking sheet.

2 Heat the oil in a large saucepan. Add the corn, cover with a lid and cook over a low heat until all the corn has popped, discarding any unpopped corn.

3 Add the corn to the chocolate with the sesame seeds, dates and apples. Stir until well blended.

4 Divide the popcorn mixture between the paper cases and decorate each with a few chocolate curls.

TOP & BOTTOM: Coco toffee bites;
CENTRE: Chocolate corn cups.

Chapter 5

SWEETS

— and —

FINISHING TOUCHES

This chapter has an enticing selection of chocolates with assorted flavoured centres. These include tiny cups swirled with creamy fillings; clusters of nuts and fruit coated in plain (dark) or white chocolate, and assorted truffles finished with different coatings. All these chocolates look marvellous packed into small boxes as gifts, or arranged on a plate and served to round off a dinner party. Moulded chocolates and chocolate Easter eggs are easily made in pre-formed plastic moulds — available in a variety of finishes from most kitchen shops. Chocolate decorations make perfect finishing touches for cakes, gâteaux and desserts. Use up leftover melted chocolate to make them and store in a box in a cool dry place.

CRUNCHY NUT BITES

MAKES 30

A good way to use up leftover chocolate by simply adding any mixture of nuts or fruit.

30 g (1 oz/¼ cup) skinned hazelnuts
30 g (1 oz/¼ cup) blanched almonds
30 g (1 oz/¼ cup) pecans or walnuts
30 g (1 oz/¼ cup) raisins
30 g (1 oz/2 tablespoons) stem ginger, chopped
125 g (4 oz) plain (dark), milk (semi-sweet) or white chocolate, melted
icing (confectioner's) sugar or cocoa for dusting

1 Preheat the grill. Place the nuts on a baking sheet and toast under the grill, turning occasionally, until evenly browned. Chop roughly.

2 Mix the nuts, raisins and ginger together in a bowl.

3 Add to the melted chocolate and stir until evenly blended.

4 Arrange 30 paper sweet cases on a baking sheet and place a heaped teaspoonful of mixture in each.

5 Leave to set, then dust with icing (confectioner's) sugar, or cocoa if white chocolate is used.

RUM TRUFFLES

MAKES 50

These truffles may be flavoured with spirits or liqueurs if you prefer. Alternative coatings are melted chocolate, chopped nuts and desiccated coconut.

85 ml (3 fl oz/⅓ cup) whipping cream
3 tablespoons dark rum
60 g (2 oz) plain (dark) chocolate, melted
60 g (2 oz) milk (semi-sweet) chocolate, melted
125 g (4 oz) white chocolate, melted
COATINGS
2 tablespoons plain (dark) chocolate strands
1 tablespoon cocoa powder
1 tablespoon icing (confectioner's) sugar, sieved
60 g (2 oz) white chocolate, grated

1 Heat the cream until hot but not boiling. Stir in the rum and add one third to each of the bowls of melted chocolate; stir until smooth. Allow to cool slightly, stirring occasionally, until thick enough to mould.

2 Using a teaspoon, divide the plain (dark) chocolate mixture into about 15 spoonfuls, placing them on a sheet of non-stick paper. Shape each piece into a neat ball and roll in chocolate strands to coat evenly. Leave in a cool place to set.

3 Repeat to make milk (semi-sweet) chocolate truffles: shape the mixture into 15 balls and coat in cocoa mixed with icing (confectioner's) sugar.

4 Shape the white chocolate into 20 neat balls and roll in grated chocolate.

TOP: Crunchy nut bites; BOTTOM: Rum truffles

EASY CHOCOLATES

MAKES 18

Simply buy a plastic tray of moulded chocolate shapes and fill with white chocolate and your choice of fillings. Tint the melted chocolate pale pink or green with powdered food colourings if you prefer.

250 g (8 oz) white chocolate, melted
FILLINGS
1 piece of stem ginger, chopped
1 tablespoon chocolate hazelnut spread
2 dried apricots, chopped
TO FINISH
30 g (1 oz) plain (dark) chocolate, melted

1 Polish the inside of the chocolate moulds with cotton wool so they are really clean.

2 Fill with white chocolate, leave for 5 seconds, then pour excess chocolate back into the bowl. Draw a palette knife across the top of the tray to neaten the edges of the chocolate cases, then invert on to a baking sheet lined with non-stick paper and chill for 2 minutes.

3 Spoon a little ginger into one third of the cases. Spoon chocolate spread into a further third. Divide the apricot between the rest. Cover the fillings with the remaining white chocolate, to the top of the moulds.

4 Chill to set the chocolate. Invert the tray and press the tops to release the chocolates.

5 To finish, pipe contrasting threads of plain (dark) chocolate on top of the sweets. Leave to set.

MARZIPAN CHERRY CHOCOLATES

MAKES 20

Surprise chocolates flavoured with maraschino and crème de menthe — an inexpensive way to make liqueur chocolates.

10 maraschino flavoured cherries
10 crème de menthe flavoured cherries
125 g (4 oz) white marzipan
125 g (4 oz) milk (semi-sweet) chocolate, melted
125 g (4 oz) plain (dark) chocolate, melted
30 g (1 oz) white chocolate, melted

1 Drain the cherries, keeping them separate, and dry on kitchen paper.

2 Cut the marzipan into 20 pieces and roll each piece to a circle on a surface lightly dusted with icing (confectioner's) sugar. Cover each cherry with a marzipan circle and roll into a neat ball.

3 Using a dipping fork, dip each maraschino cherry into the melted milk chocolate, turning to coat evenly Lift out and tap the fork on the side of the bowl to allow the excess chocolate to fall. Place the marzipan cherries on non-stick paper.

4 Repeat with the crème de menthe cherries and melted plain (dark) chocolate, to coat evenly.

5 Using a teaspoon, drizzle a little white chocolate over each cherry. Leave to set.

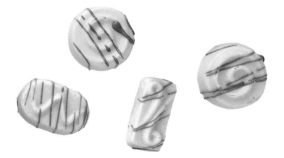

TOP & BOTTOM: Easy chocolates; CENTRE: Marzipan cherry chocolates.

NOISETTE CUPS

MAKES 20

Use plain (dark) or white chocolate for the cups and fillings and mix and match to suit your own taste. If using white chocolate for the filling, halve the quantities of brandy and cream. For a non-alcoholic version, replace the brandy with orange juice.

*125 g (4 oz) plain (dark) or white chocolate,
    melted*
FILLING
4 tablespoons whipping cream
2 tablespoons apricot brandy
1 teaspoon chopped pistachio nuts

1 Arrange 20 foil sweet cases on a baking sheet and place a teaspoonful of melted chocolate in each. Using a fine paintbrush, coat the inside of each case evenly with chocolate. Invert on to the baking sheet.

2 Place the chocolate cases in the refrigerator for 2 minutes to set quickly.

3 To make the filling, stir the melted chocolate, cream and apricot brandy together in a bowl until evenly blended. Allow to cool, stirring occasionally, until the mixture is thick enough to hold its own shape.

4 Spoon or pipe a swirl of chocolate filling into each chocolate case. Sprinkle with chopped nuts and leave to set. Peel off the foil cases if preferred.

CANDIED FRUIT CLUSTERS

MAKES 15

Use any mixture of candied or glacé fruits – cherries, angelica, pineapple, etc – for these ultra quick sweets. You can, of course, use milk (semi-sweet) or plain (dark) chocolate if you prefer.

125 g (4 oz/²/₃ cup) mixed glacé fruits
finely grated rind of 1 lime
90 g (3 oz) white chocolate, melted

1 Roughly chop the glacé fruits and place in a bowl. Stir in the finely grated lime rind until well blended.

2 Add the fruit mixture to the melted chocolate and stir well to coat evenly.

3 Arrange 15 paper sweet cases on a baking sheet and place teaspoonfuls of the fruit mixture in each. Leave in a cool place to set.

LEFT: Noisette cups and candied fruit clusters.

CHOCOLATE-DIPPED FRUITS

MAKES 30

Coat a variety of small fruits in season with chocolate for an attractive after-dinner treat. For contrast, use both white and plain (dark) chocolate.

selection of small fruits, eg grapes, raspberries, strawberries, redcurrants, blueberries, kumquats, blackberries, cherries
155 g (5 oz) plain (dark), milk (semi-sweet) or white chocolate, melted
TO DECORATE
fresh fruit leaves

1 Select firm fruits with the stems or hulls intact. Carefully wipe clean with kitchen paper if necessary.

2 Line 2 baking sheets with baking parchment.

3 Hold a piece of fruit by the stem or tip and partially dip into the melted chocolate to half-coat.

4 Allow the excess chocolate to fall into the bowl, then place the fruit on the paper-lined baking sheets.

5 Repeat with remaining fruit and leave in a cool place to set.

6 Arrange dipped fruits on serving plates and decorate with fruit leaves.

CHOCOLATE MINT STICKS

MAKES 30

Serve these as an after-dinner treat. Ready-to-roll icing is great for a quick fondant filling. Flavour it with grated orange, lemon or lime zest if you prefer.

125 g (4 oz) ready-to-roll icing
4 drops peppermint oil
125 g (4 oz) plain (dark) or milk (semi-sweet) chocolate, melted

1 Press the ready-to-roll icing flat, using your fingers. Add a few drops of peppermint oil and knead the icing until smooth and free from cracks.

2 Roll out the icing on a surface lightly dusted with icing (confectioner's) sugar to a 20 x 6 cm (8 x 2½ in) rectangle. Trim the edges to neaten.

3 Using a sharp knife, cut the fondant across the short width into 5 mm (¼ in) sticks. Separate each stick, keeping them straight and even.

4 Meanwhile, line a baking sheet with baking parchment.

5 Using a fine brush, coat the underside of each mint stick with chocolate and place on the paper, chocolate side down.

6 Brush the sticks with melted chocolate to coat completely. Leave to set, then peel away the paper.

TOP: Chocolate-dipped fruits; BOTTOM: Chocolate mint sticks.

DIPPED CHOCOLATES

MAKES 26-28

Simply dip nuts, glacé fruits, marzipan, fondant, etc, into milk (semi-sweet), plain (dark) or white chocolate.

30 g (1 oz) white marzipan
2 teaspoons rosewater or grated lemon rind
60 g (2 oz) ready-to-roll icing
185 g (6 oz) milk (semi-sweet), plain (dark) or
*   white chocolate, melted*
4 ratafia biscuits (cookies)
4 brazil nuts
4 stoned dates
COATINGS & TOPPINGS
1 teaspoon chopped pistachio nuts
crystallized rose petals

1 Shape the marzipan into 16 tiny balls and arrange in clusters of four, pressing together lightly.

2 Knead the rosewater or rind into the ready-to-roll icing. Roll out to a 1 cm (½ in) thickness and cut out 10-12 shapes.

3 Using a dipping fork, dip the marzipan clusters into the chocolate, turning to coat evenly. Lift out and tap the fork on the side of the bowl to allow the excess chocolate to fall. Place the chocolates on non-stick paper.

4 Dip the fondant shapes, ratafias, brazil nuts and dates in the same way.

5 Top nut chocolates with pistachios, and other chocolates with crystallized petals; or pipe contrasting chocolate over some of the sweets. Allow chocolates to dry.

SIMPLE EASTER EGGS

MAKES 3

These are easy to make in plastic trays which have 6 egg half moulds.

250 g (8 oz) plain (dark), milk (semi-sweet) or
*   white chocolate, melted*
30 g (1 oz) ready-to-roll icing
pink, blue and yellow food colourings

1 Polish 6 small Easter egg moulds with cotton wool to ensure they are really clean.

2 Fill each mould with chocolate, leave for a few minutes, then pour excess chocolate back into the bowl. Draw a palette knife across the top of the moulds to neaten the edges. Invert moulds on to non-stick paper and chill for 2 minutes.

3 Repeat this process twice to give 3 layers of chocolate. Leave in a cool place to set.

4 Gently press top of moulds to release eggs. Brush edges with melted chocolate and stick egg halves together in pairs.

5 Cut ready-to-roll icing into 3 pieces. Tint portions pale pink, blue and yellow, using a few drops of colouring.

6 Roll out each piece thinly on a surface lightly dusted with icing (confectioner's) sugar. Using cutters, cut out bunnies and flowers.

7 Attach bunnies and flowers to eggs with a little melted chocolate. Pack into boxes or baskets.

RIGHT: Dipped chocolates and simple Easter eggs.

Chocolate Boxes

MAKES 2

Fill these delightful boxes with chocolates, truffles or dipped fruits.

125 g (4 oz) plain (dark) chocolate, melted
60 g (2 oz) white chocolate, melted

1 Line a baking sheet with baking parchment.

2 Pour the plain (dark) chocolate over the paper-lined baking sheet and spread evenly with a palette knife to a 15 x 12 cm (5 x 7 in) rectangle. Pick up the two top corners of the paper and drop several times to level the chocolate and smooth the surface.

3 Using a teaspoon, drizzle some of the white chocolate evenly over the surface to give a marbled effect. Leave until the chocolate is almost set but still pliable.

4 Lay a clean piece of baking parchment over the surface and invert the chocolate on to it. Peel the paper off the back of the chocolate and turn the chocolate over.

5 Using a ruler and sharp knife, cut eight 4 cm (1½ in) squares for the sides and four 4.5 cm (1 ¾ in) squares for the bases and lids.

6 To assemble boxes, brush the edges of 4 side pieces and the upper edges of 1 base piece with melted chocolate. Position the side pieces on the base, pressing the edges together to form a box. Leave to set. Repeat to make another box.

7 Fill with chocolates or dipped fruits and place lid in position.

Chocolate Baskets

MAKES 4

These attractive baskets make ideal containers for ice cream, fruit and whipped cream, chocolates, or sugar-frosted fruits or flowers.

125 g (4 oz) plain (dark) chocolate, melted

1 Place a bun tin (pan) or chosen basket-shaped moulds in the freezer to chill thoroughly.

2 Half-fill a greaseproof (waxed) paper piping bag with melted chocolate and snip off the tip.

3 Drizzle the chocolate thread backwards and forwards over the outside of the chilled shapes until evenly covered, making sure the top edge has a continuous rim of chocolate. Return to the freezer until set hard.

4 Tap the inside of the moulds sharply to release the chocolate baskets. Fill with ice cream scoops, chocolates, dipped fruits or sugar frosted flowers.

VARIATION
To make simple chocolate baskets, brush the insides of paper cake cases evenly with melted chocolate. Leave until set, then apply a second coat. When the chocolate has set, carefully peel away the paper.

TOP: Chocolate boxes; CENTRE & BOTTOM: Chocolate baskets.

CHOCOLATE CURLS

MAKES 24

Always an eye-catching decoration for that extra special touch.

125 g (4 oz) plain (dark), milk (semi-sweet) or white chocolate, melted

1 Pour the melted chocolate on to a rigid work surface, preferably marble. Using a large palette knife, spread it evenly backwards and forwards to obtain a smooth, level finish.

2 When the chocolate has just set, but not hard, make the curls. Hold a medium-sized sharp knife at a 45° angle to the chocolate and draw the knife towards you across the surface of the chocolate to remove thin layers that form into long curls. Place on a baking sheet lined with non-stick paper and keep in a cool place until required.

3 Quick chocolate curls may be made by using a potato peeler to shave short curls off a block of milk (semi-sweet), plain (dark) or white chocolate. For best results, have the chocolate at room temperature; if the chocolate is cold, it will not curl.

CHOCOLATE CUT-OUTS

Simple, effective cut-out chocolate shapes — ideal for decorating desserts, gâteaux and cakes. Drizzle white chocolate over plain (dark) chocolate to give a marbled effect.

60 g (2 oz) plain (dark), milk (semi-sweet) or white chocolate, melted

1 Line a baking sheet with baking parchment.

2 Pour the chocolate over the paper-lined baking sheet and spread evenly with a palette knife. Pick up the top two corners of the paper and drop several times to level the chocolate and smooth the surface.

3 Leave the chocolate until it is just set. To test, touch the edges: they should not feel sticky. Lay a clean piece of baking parchment over the surface and invert the chocolate on to it. Peel the paper off the back of the chocolate and turn the chocolate over. Take care to avoid touching the shiny surface of the cut-out or it will become dull.

4 Using small plain or fancy cutters, cut out chocolate shapes carefully before the chocolate sets hard and becomes brittle.

5 For the chocolate squares and triangles, use a ruler and sharp knife to measure and cut out the shapes.

6 Store flat on a tray lined with kitchen paper in a cool place.

LEFT: Chocolate curls, chocolate cut-outs, chocolate leaves (see page 94) and piped chocolate decorations (see page 94).

CHOCOLATE LEAVES

MAKES 12

Choose any firm leaves in good condition with well-defined veins, but don't use ivy leaves or other poisonous ones. Make chocolate leaves in advance, store in a cool, dry place and use as required for decorating all kinds of desserts, sweets and cakes.

selection of leaves, eg rose, red- or blackcurrant, nasturtium, herb, or lemon leaves on a short stem
60 g (2 oz) plain (dark), white or milk (semi-sweet) chocolate, melted

1 Line a baking sheet with baking parchment. Wipe the leaves with kitchen paper and ensure they are perfectly clean and dry.

2 Using a paintbrush, thickly coat the underside of each leaf with melted chocolate. Take care to avoid painting over the edge of leaves as this will prevent them being peeled away cleanly.

3 Place each leaf a little apart on the baking parchment with the chocolate side uppermost. Leave in a cool place to set.

4 Carefully peel the leaves away from the chocolate.

5 Use to decorate cakes, desserts, ice creams and gâteaux.

PIPED CHOCOLATE DECORATIONS

A good way to use up leftover chocolate. Simply pipe designs of your choice and keep in an airtight container for standby decorations.

2 tablespoons milk (semi-sweet), plain (dark) or white chocolate, melted

1 Draw your chosen design as many times as required on a piece of plain paper and secure to a flat surface with sticky tape. Place a piece of non-stick paper on top. Half-fill a greaseproof (waxed) paper piping bag with melted chocolate and fold down the top. Snip off the tip of the bag. Pipe a fine thread of chocolate, following the design.

2 Alternatively, pipe free-hand designs directly on to the paper and allow to dry.

3 Slide a fine palette knife underneath the chocolate pieces to release them.

NOTE
To make a greaseproof (waxed) paper piping bag, fold a square of greaseproof paper into a small triangle. Hold the folded edge away from you with the opposite point in front. Take the right hand point and fold it to the centre point in front of you. Hold these two points together to form a cone shape. Take the left point over the cone and bring all the points together at the back. Fold the points inwards to secure the bag.

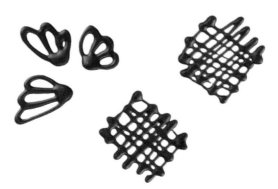

INDEX

The page numbers in *italics* refer to photographs